101 DILEMMAS for the ARMCHAIR PHILOSOPHER

Quarto is the authority on a wide range of topics.
Quarto educates, entertains and enriches the lives of
our readers—enthusiasts and lovers of hands-on living.
www.QuartoKnows.com

Published by Quad Books
Copyright © 2017 Quid Publishing
Conceived, designed and produced by
Quid Publishing
an imprint of The Quarto Group
Level One
Ovest House
58 West Street
Brighton
BN1 2RA
England

ISBN: 978-0-85762-506-9

Design by Tony Seddon
Illustrations by Matthew Windsor

Printed in China

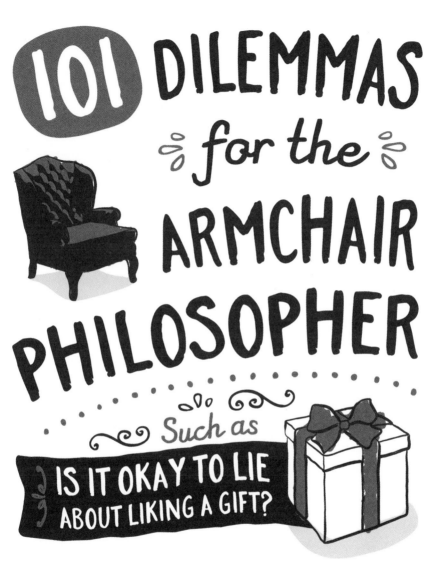

101 DILEMMAS for the ARMCHAIR PHILOSOPHER

Such as

IS IT OKAY TO LIE ABOUT LIKING A GIFT?

ERIC CHALINE

QUAD BOOKS

CONTENTS

INTRODUCTION

'A person may cause evil to others not only by his actions but by his inaction, and in either case he is justly accountable to them for the injury.'
– John Stuart Mill (1806–1873)

Say the word 'philosopher', and you might picture an ancient Greek sage wrestling with metaphysics and aesthetics, an eighteenth-century savant putting quill to paper to discuss the doctrine of natural rights, or a bespectacled public intellectual dissecting the finer points of linguistics and epistemology. And though it is true that much of philosophy concerns itself with the obscure, abstruse and abstract, there is a very practical branch of the subject that we all use in our daily lives: ethics. When we make judgements about how we or other people should behave in certain situations, we are making ethical judgements, choosing one of the three approaches: one that looks at the character and intent of the moral agent (virtue ethics), one that looks at an action in terms of its adherence to a set of rules (deontological ethics), and one that evaluates the morality of an action from its consequences (consequentialist ethics).

Our ethical decisions are not just for the big issues such as capital punishment, abortion and gay marriage, but also for very mundane questions, such as 'Should I buy fair trade or go for the cheapest brand?' Or 'Should I give the homeless person a few pounds or are there more effective ways of helping the disadvantaged in our society?' At less frequent intervals, through elections and referenda, we are asked to make decisions about much bigger problems that will affect not only ourselves and the people around us, but potentially our entire country, region or the whole world.

How to use this book

The 101 dilemmas are divided into eleven themed chapters, covering every aspect of personal and public life. Each dilemma is illustrated by a short scenario, with additional explanatory materials, including thought experiments, analogies and quotes, that explain the approaches that philosophers have devised to resolve them. Many of the topics are so complex that it would be impossible to mention all the ethical issues that they raise. This book is intended not as a comprehensive guide to moral philosophy, but as a starting point for an investigation of ethics.

I have rarely included approaches from closed ethical systems such as Christianity, Judaism or Islam (unless an aspect of faith itself is the subject of the dilemma), because these belief systems do not admit the existence of ethical uncertainties. They prescribe a right answer to any given problem. In the case of abortion, for example, a fundamentalist or Catholic Christian will always say that the sacredness of life trumps all other considerations. This book has not been written to give the readers pat answers to complex human problems, but to equip them with some of the philosophical tools that will help them to make informed ethical decisions about issues both great and small.

'Act in such a way that you treat humanity, whether in your own person or in the person of any other, never merely as a _means_ to an _end_, but always at the same time as an _end_.'
– **Immanuel Kant (1724–1804)**

PERSONAL

'No man is an island, entire of itself;
every man is a piece of the continent,
a part of the main.'
– John Donne (1572–1631)

001 MILE-HIGH MANNERS

Bill is on a flight with his wife and two small children, Tina, eight, and Matt, ten. A young couple across the aisle are drinking and talking loudly. Bill looks over at his wife, Cindy, and rolls his eyes as if to say: 'Kids today!' She, however, obviously wants him to say something. Luckily for Bill, the passenger behind the couple stands up and asks them to 'Keep it down', which they do.

Later, however, the couple start to get 'friendly' under an airline blanket. No one looking at them could be in any doubt that they are engaging in behaviour that would be considered inappropriate in a public place. Bill smiles and thinks, 'Get a room'. Cindy is less than amused, but the man who intervened earlier cannot see what they are doing and is unlikely to complain this time. Tina and Matt are asleep, but they might wake up and see what the couple are doing. Bill isn't offended but Cindy clearly is, and, of course, he has to think about Tina and Matt and the example the couple are setting for them. Should he say something or call the flight attendant?

Taking liberties

That great defender of individual liberty, John Stuart Mill, stated that the only laws that could be imposed on free citizens by force were those that prevent harm to others. The case for laws against murder, rape and theft, in which the 'harm to others' is clear, is easy to make. But what about breaches of 'good manners'?

You would think that Mill, with his definition of harm, might consider that a person who is rude, inconsiderate or even indecent in public could not and should not be censured for their behaviour, let alone be subject to forceful interference. But as you can see from the quote reproduced on the next page, while Mill had no concerns about a person's manners in private, in public he agreed that any violations of 'good manners' did fall into the category of 'offences against others'. Is Mill being hypocritical, inconsistent or putting forward a more nuanced view of 'harm'?

Bill has to balance the rights of the young couple to privacy against the offence they are causing to his wife and the potential harm to his kids.

MANNERS: ARE THEY SIMPLY OUTMODED CONVENTIONS THAT SHOULD BE DONE AWAY WITH, OR THE OIL THAT LUBRICATES SOCIAL INTERACTIONS AND PREVENTS SOCIETY FROM DEGENERATING INTO CHAOS?

'There are many acts which, being directly injurious only to the agents themselves, ought not to be legally interdicted, but which, if done publicly, are a violation of good manners, and coming within the category of offences against others, may rightly be prohibited.'
– John Stuart Mill

002 THE VALUE OF A LATTE

Sally's job doesn't pay a lot; she can't afford many luxuries. But every day on her way home, she treats herself to a large latte from the local coffee shop. It's a bit expensive, but to Sally it's worth every cent.

One evening on her way home, she gets to talking to a charity collector, who tells her that for the price of a latte, she could pay for treatment that would save someone's eyesight in the developing world. When she weighs the loss of her own fleeting pleasure against the loss of another person's sight, she feels obliged to forgo that evening's latte and gives the money to charity. As she walks past the coffee shop, she feels a moment's regret about losing her treat, but she's also glad she's done the 'right thing'.

The next evening, the charity collector isn't there. But Sally can't help thinking that if he had been, she could have given up her latte again to save another person's eyesight. When she passes the coffee shop, she stops and looks thoughtfully through the window, asking herself whether she'll ever be able to enjoy her latte as she did before.

> WE ALL LIKE TO TREAT OURSELVES FROM TIME TO TIME, BUT ISN'T THERE ALWAYS SOMETHING MORE WORTHWHILE WE COULD BE DOING WITH OUR MONEY?

Buddy, can you spare me a ... latte?

Contemporary Australian philosopher Peter Singer says that those who are financially secure have a moral duty to reduce poverty and to relieve its effects. He says:

'... the failure of people in the rich nations to make any significant sacrifices in order to assist people who are dying from poverty-related causes is ethically indefensible. It is not simply the absence of charity, let alone of moral saintliness. It is wrong, and one cannot claim to be a morally decent person unless one is doing far more than the typical comfortably-off person does.'

His argument, essentially, is that if it is within our power to alleviate significant suffering at comparably little cost to ourselves then we ought to do it. Is this a reasonable argument? If not, why not?

Thought experiment: the drowning child

Imagine that you are walking past a lake and see a drowning child. The lake isn't deep, so you know you can rescue the child at no risk to your own life. However, the water is filthy, and you are wearing an expensive suit. What should you do?

Clearly you have a moral obligation to save the child, since the life of the child is of incomparably greater value than your suit.

Thought experiment: the trachoma patient

You are visiting a hospital in a developing country and you meet a child who is suffering from trachoma: an eye infection that can become agonisingly painful and lead to blindness. Unfortunately, the hospital has used up all of its supplies of the appropriate antibiotic and does not have the funds to buy any more. But for a small amount of cash – no more than the price of a cup of coffee back home – you could buy a single-dose pill that will cure the infection.

Do you have a moral obligation to buy it? Doesn't Sally face essentially the same choice every evening?

003 PRIVATE ACTS, PUBLIC HARM

Marcel has been growing marijuana for his personal use for the past ten years. He occasionally gives or sells some to friends, but he does not depend on the income. However, while the law in his country allows people to have a small amount of cannabis for personal use, there are serious penalties for those in possession of larger amounts or who are found to be dealing. In the eyes of the law, Marcel is committing a crime. In his own mind, however, Marcel thinks he's one of the good guys, especially since he started giving some of his produce to his mother, who suffers from a type of arthritis that cannot be alleviated with prescription medication.

Marcel sells to his friends Lou and Melissa, whom he's known since his university days. They are not stereotypical 'stoners' – they have good jobs and a four-year-old son, Josh, and only smoke recreationally. One evening, Marcel gets a panicked call from Lou. Josh somehow got hold of their stash of marijuana and ate the whole packet. He had convulsions and then passed out cold.

The law would criminalise Marcel as the dealer and, to a lesser extent, the parents as users. But who has allowed the harm? Marcel, by growing the marijuana and selling it to Lou and Melissa, or the parents, by leaving the drug where their son could find it?

'Drunkenness, for example, in ordinary cases, is not a fit subject for legislative interference.... The making himself drunk, in a person whom drunkenness excites to do harm to others, is a crime against others.'
— **John Stuart Mill**

Thought experiment: legalise or ban?

Imagine two towns: In 'Hightown' drugs are legal, controlled substances, manufactured by scientists to have minimal side effects. The whole town is set up to minimise the risks to anyone on drugs, with medics on call, free addiction services and 'chill-out' zones in public places. The neighbouring 'Badtripville' is the exact opposite: Drugs are illegal and sold by gangs who don't care about their purity and side effects. Addiction is a major problem, leading to crimes and muggings; and death rates from overdoses and impure drugs are high.

The current situation in the developed world is somewhere between these two extremes, with bans and criminal sanctions alongside more permissive legislation and treatment as an alternative to criminalisation. But even in Hightown, with its enlightened approach to the use of drugs to minimise their harm, there will be cases like Josh's, in which unintended harm is caused by the availability of drugs.

MANY PEOPLE BELIEVE THAT PRIVATE ACTIONS, EVEN CRIMINAL ACTIONS, THAT DO NOT INVOLVE THE PUBLIC REALM ARE 'VICTIMLESS CRIMES'. THEY DO NOT CAUSE HARM TO A THIRD PARTY. BUT CAN A PRIVATE ACT DO PUBLIC HARM?

004 FAIR TRADE TRADE-OFF

Marcia is doing the weekly grocery run at her local supermarket. With a family of six to feed, she usually opts for economy products. This week, however, her husband Jerry finally got his long-overdue promotion, along with a welcome pay rise, and Marcia feels she can be a bit more generous with her purchases now. She stops in the fresh produce aisle to load up on bananas, which the kids love. Just past the regular bananas, she notices another banana display under a sign emblazoned with 'Fair-trade bananas – make a difference!' alongside a picture of a smiling farmer and his family. They look exactly like the bananas she usually buys but they are about 30 percent more expensive. It's only a few pounds extra on the week's shopping costs, which Marcia works out would cost her £100 to £150 more a year.

Marcia has heard about fair trade, which guarantees that farmers get a fair price for their crop, rather than all the profit going to the big fruit companies, wholesalers and supermarkets. Advocates of fair trade also claim that it promotes sustainable development, leading to improved social and environmental conditions, which are a clear benefit not just to the producer but to the whole world. In a way, by choosing fair trade, Marcia is helping herself, her family and the planet.

'Really, £150 is not a lot for me', she thinks. 'But to the family in the picture, it's probably the money to send their kids to school or buy new farm machinery.' With her mind made up, she wheels her shopping cart over to the fair-trade display. But will her act of generosity make the difference that the sign claims it will?

Heart strings over purse strings

Readers might think that Marcia's choice relates more to economics than ethics, and to an extent they would be right. In this example, is the price difference a deciding factor in whether Marcia chooses fair trade? For Marcia, as for many of us, it may well be. If the bananas were 50 percent more expensive, would she still buy them? And if they had been just 10 percent more last week, would she have bought them before? Here, Marcia is motivated by the thought that her financial circumstances have improved, and she can therefore allow herself a choice that goes against her economic interests but makes her feel that, in a small way, she is making a difference for the better.

THE BENEFITS OF BUYING FAIR-TRADE PRODUCE ARE MUCH TOUTED, BUT SOME ARGUE THAT IT IS FAR FROM FAIR FOR THE MAJORITY OF PRODUCERS IN THE DEVELOPING WORLD. WILL THE WORLD REALLY BE A BETTER PLACE IF WE CHOOSE FAIR TRADE?

Is free fairer than fair?

Opponents of the fair-trade system argue that, in buying the bananas, Marcia is actually causing more harm than good, through faulty ethical reasoning. In a world where fair trade has to compete with free trade, the distortions of the market it creates enrich some farmers but at the cost of beggaring others. For fair trade to be truly fair, the principle would have to be applied equally to all farmers across the developing world so that their produce competed on equal terms.

005 DEADLY CHOICES

Anna-Lise is approaching her seventy-fifth birthday. She is independent and in reasonable health but often feels lonely. She is divorced and never had children. Her siblings have predeceased her and she is not close to any of her surviving kin. Many of her close friends have died. Life has lost its savour. Without any strong religious beliefs to hold her back, she is seriously considering whether now might not be the time to bow out gracefully, before she falls seriously ill or becomes incapacitated.

She has not told anyone about wanting to die because she thinks most people would misunderstand. Her young doctor, for example, would think that she is depressed and prescribe pills or therapy; the staff at the senior centre she attends would think some scheming relatives were trying to get their hands on her money.

It is not a lack of will holding Anna-Lise back, but a lack of reliable means. In her jurisdiction it is illegal for anyone to aid or abet a suicide, and, not being terminally ill, she does not qualify under the limited number of exemptions that do allow for assisted suicide. She also has to consider that her suicide might harm an innocent bystander. Worse still, what if she botched the attempt and ended up in the incapacitated state she was trying to avoid? If only there was a guaranteed instant, painless pill she could take.

With an ageing population in the developed world, we are likely to get many people like Anna-Lise, who want the right to decide when they should die, in the same way as younger people decide when they should have children.

Death control

The sanctity-of-life arguments put forward by members of faith communities are too well-known to repeat here. The opposing case was clearly set out by American philosopher and psychiatrist Thomas Szasz (1920–2012), who equated the individual's right to die with an individual's right to practise birth control. Szasz was an outspoken critic of state interference in the private lives of citizens, coining the term the 'therapeutic state' in 1963 to expose what he saw as characterisation of unconventional actions, thoughts and beliefs as psychiatric illnesses to be 'cured'. Among these, he included the rational decision to commit suicide, which he argued was not an issue that should concern either the state or the psychiatric profession.

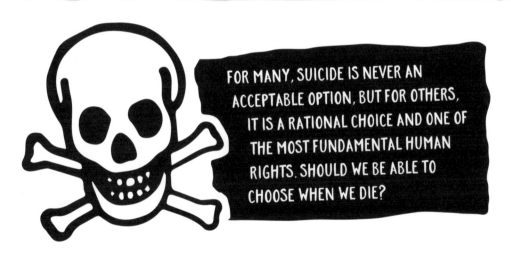

FOR MANY, SUICIDE IS NEVER AN ACCEPTABLE OPTION, BUT FOR OTHERS, IT IS A RATIONAL CHOICE AND ONE OF THE MOST FUNDAMENTAL HUMAN RIGHTS. SHOULD WE BE ABLE TO CHOOSE WHEN WE DIE?

'Suicide is not the ultimate exercise of freedom but its ultimate self-contradiction: a free act that by destroying life, destroys all the individual's earthly freedom.'
– **Richard Doerflinger**

⚘006 UNLUCKY FOR SOME

Tom and Bob are driving home from their weekly game at the local golf club, each driving his own car. By some freak coincidence, the brakes on Tom's sedan and Bob's SUV fail at exactly the same moment (no, their wives were not seen with bolt cutters anywhere near the golf club moments before they drove off). Unable to stop, Tom speeds through a red light at an intersection, narrowly missing a pedestrian who is young and nimble enough to jump out of the way. Unfortunately, the pedestrian jumps directly into the path of Bob's SUV. The young man is killed instantly. The police arrive at the scene of the accident and interview the drivers and witnesses and check the traffic cameras at the intersection. Bob is immediately arrested on a charge of reckless driving and faces an indictment for manslaughter. Tom, on the other hand, is issued with a traffic violation for going through the red light.

Both drivers experienced exactly the same circumstances: the sudden failure of their brakes, which caused them to go through a red light. The men had not planned for their brakes to fail at that moment, nor to go through a red light when a pedestrian was crossing. But if the two men are found to be negligent, the law will consider that Bob is morally much more culpable than Tom, even though it was only down to luck that Bob was driving behind Tom.

WE ARE ALL THOUGHT TO BE IN CHARGE OF OUR OWN ACTIONS, BUT CAN WE BE HELD MORALLY RESPONSIBLE FOR SITUATIONS THAT ARE OUTSIDE OF OUR CONTROL?

Thought experiment: Gaugin's gamble

The concept of 'moral luck', which is illustrated by Tom and Bob's rather unlikely story, was first introduced by British philosopher Bernard Williams (1929–2003), who fully expected the idea 'to suggest an oxymoron', that is, the conjunction of two contradictory terms, rendering both meaningless. We associate the term 'moral' with voluntary actions under our rational control, while luck is very much something out of our control. Williams suggested the following thought experiment to illustrate moral luck, which he based loosely on the life of the French painter Paul Gauguin (1848–1903).

Gaugin abandons his home and family for the South Seas in a bid to become a world-famous artist. There are two possible outcomes: He becomes a great painter or is a dismal failure. Williams argues that our moral assessment of Gaugin's flight to Tahiti will be very different depending on whether he succeeds or fails. The painter himself, though he believes in his talent, cannot be certain that he will succeed, which is dependent in part on circumstances outside of his control – in other words, luck – yet many might give him moral credit for his success (or moral blame for his failure). In reality Gauguin was lucky – a beneficiary of moral good luck, in the same way that Bob was the victim of moral bad luck.

'Williams takes himself to be challenging not just Kantian thinking about morality, but also commonplace ideas about it. He claims the idea that morality is immune to luck is "basic to our ideas of morality".'

– Judith Andre

⸲007 HAPPY GROUCH

Mark is sitting on a park bench with his elderly neighbour Jim one lunchtime. Mark looks so downcast that Jim asks him if anything is wrong. At first, Mark is unwilling to engage in a conversation, but he gradually opens up. 'I've tried everything,' he says plaintively to Jim, who is placidly eating his sandwiches. 'But I never seem to be happy. My friend Sam, he runs marathons for fun. But when I went running with him, I was bored and got cramp and had to limp home. Another friend, Will, collects stamps, but when I spent an afternoon with him, looking at his collection and scanning the online auctions, he got all excited when he won a bid for a one-penny stamp, and all I thought was, 'It's just a piece of paper with Queen Victoria on it. Who cares if it's worth £1 or £100!"

Mark tells Jim that he has a shelf full of books by 'so-called happiness experts' but that they are all just nonsense. 'Oh, yeah, the authors are happy, because dumb saps like me buy their books and make them money!' Jim patiently sits and nods as Mark runs through a litany of complaints, talking animatedly about his life, his apartment, his job, his girlfriend, his family, his prospects, the state of the economy, the political system and the price of a decent latte, until Mark has run out of things to complain about. Jim puts down his sandwich and looks thoughtfully at the younger man, who was so downcast and detached from his surroundings a few minutes before, but is now excited, alive, engaged with the world, albeit in a rather negative way. 'How do you feel now, son?' Jim asks. Mark is about to say that he's as miserable as ever, but he's not. He stands up and looks around. It is the same park, but somehow everything looks slightly different. Suddenly full of energy, he strides purposefully off towards his office.

Jim smiles to himself, thinking, 'Seems that some people are only happy when they're miserable.'

IT CAN SEEM THAT HAPPINESS IS THE ULTIMATE GOAL OF MODERN LIFE BUT DO WE REALLY UNDERSTAND WHAT IT MEANS TO BE HAPPY? DO SOME PEOPLE FIND HAPPINESS IN BEING MISERABLE?

The paradox of hedonism

Philosophers since Aristotle (384–322 BCE) have argued that the active pursuit of pleasure and happiness is the one sure-fire way of not being happy – the so-called 'pleasure paradox'. John Stuart Mill wrote in his autobiography, 'Ask yourself whether you are happy, and you cease to be so'.

When Mark saw Sam and Will enjoying marathon running and stamp collecting, he confused the pursuit of these hobbies for the pleasure and happiness they brought them. There is nothing intrinsically pleasurable about running or stamp collecting, but for those who are fully engaged in such pursuits, they are an indirect source of happiness. Mill would point out that for Sam and Will, 'Aiming thus at something else, they find happiness along the way'. The paradox of Mark is that he is able to find his own brand of happiness by being a grouch.

SOCIAL

'The first step in the evolution of ethics is a sense of solidarity with other human beings.'
– Albert Schweitzer (1875–1965)

⸮008 LITTLE WHITE LIES

Early on Christmas morning Andrew takes out the stacks of presents from their hiding place. He isn't a minute too soon. Moments later, his five-year-old daughter Cate bursts into the room, eyes shining with excitement, and asks excitedly, 'Did Santa come?' 'Of course, he came!' Andrew replies, pointing at the brightly wrapped boxes. 'Presents don't just deliver themselves.'

Later that day, Andrew's mum arrives and presents him with an ugly hand-knitted jumper. He thanks her effusively, saying, 'It's just the thing for these cold winter days!'

After lunch, when everyone has eaten and drunk too much, Andrew enlivens the proceedings with tales of his childhood – all suitably embellished, of course.

That evening, when everyone has gone to bed, Andrew's wife, Katherine, gives his hand an affectionate squeeze. 'It's been a great day,' she says. 'That's because we had all of the essential ingredients for a great Christmas,' he replies, with a smile. 'Plenty of lights, heaps of turkey … and lots and lots of little white lies!'

CHRISTMAS! THE SEASON OF PEACE AND GOODWILL, DUPLICITY AND DECEIT. EVERY YEAR WE RECEIVE UNWANTED GIFTS. AND EVERY YEAR WE SMILE AND SAY, 'HOW LOVELY!' IS IT WRONG TO TELL THOSE LITTLE WHITE LIES?

Calculate the consequences

According to the English utilitarian philosopher Jeremy Bentham (1748–1832), in any given set of circumstances, the morally correct action is the one that is likely to bring about the greatest happiness to the greatest number of people. So when mum presents you with a hideous jumper, you should think about the probable consequences. If you tell her what you really think, you will upset her and cast a pall over the festivities. If, on the other hand, you tell her a little white lie, there will be hugs and smiles all round. By this account, it seems that lying is not only the most convenient course of action, but the right thing to do.

Do your duty

According to the German philosopher Immanuel Kant (1724–1804), morality consists of a system of duties that he calls 'categorical imperatives'. For Kant, these imperatives, or duties, apply to everyone and at all times. 'Do not lie' is one such duty. Therefore, we ought always to refrain from lying, whatever the consequences to ourselves and others.

So in Kant's view, when mum hands you a hideous jumper, duty forbids you from saying, 'What a great jumper!' You are allowed to say something diplomatic like, 'That's so kind of you, mum!' But if she asks you outright, 'Do you like it?' Kant would think that you are duty-bound to tell the truth.

'Society can exist only on the basis that there is some amount of polished lying and that no one says exactly what he thinks.'
– Lin Yutang (1895–1976)

৳009 JUST KIDDING AROUND

'A gay Jew, a black Catholic and a blind Muslim walk into a bar…' the stand-up comedian begins, and the audience braces itself for a joke that might succeed in offending six different groups: members of the LGBT community, people with disabilities and people of African heritage, as well as members of three major faith groups. The punchline might cause offence to one or all the groups mentioned – or to none, if the comedian manages to turn the clichéd joke format on its head, to make fun of the format itself.

The content and intent of the joke are not the only things we have to consider when we are deciding whether or not it is offensive. Let's take another opening line: 'A black Jew, a black Catholic and a black Muslim walk into a bar…' Would it make a difference if the comedian telling the joke were black or white? What about the racial breakdown of the audience? Who is likely to find the joke funnier – a mixed black and white audience, a black audience or a white audience? It seems to be OK for a Jewish comic to make jokes about Jews or a black comedian to make jokes about people of African heritage, but make jokes about a community of which you are not a member, and you run the risk of being accused of sexism, racism or bigotry.

ARE THERE ANY SUBJECTS THAT ARE OFF LIMITS TO COMEDIANS, OR DOES THE FREEDOM TO MAKE FUN OF SOMETHING OR SOMEONE ALWAYS TRUMP THE OFFENCE IT MIGHT CAUSE?

The limits of fun

Comedians' right to offend is coming under increasing scrutiny and pressure in many parts of the developed world. Along with the laudable aim of protecting specific groups from discrimination, persecution and hate speech comes the danger that the freedom to disagree with and make fun of certain people will also become outlawed. In recent years, there have been several incidents in which humour has triggered a violent response from the group that was targeted.

In two now-famous instances, the Prophet Muhammad was the subject of cartoons published in the Danish newspaper *Jyllands-Posten* and the French satirical magazine *Charlie Hebdo*. These contravened the Islamic ban on representations of the Prophet, and many Muslims found the content of the cartoons themselves to be offensive. In the West, the cartoons were largely considered acceptable as religious satire and their publication was defended on grounds of freedom of speech, but in the Muslim world the images caused deep offence. The consequence, in the case of the *Charlie Hebdo* cartoon, was the murder of the cartoonist and publishers of the cartoon, along with the deaths of people who had nothing to do with the cartoons but happened to be in the wrong place at the wrong time. While there is no possible justification for the actions of the murderers, were the publishers right to go ahead with publication, knowing what might happen if they did? Defenders of free speech (including myself) will be outraged at the very suggestion that they should not have been allowed to publish the images, but even the most ardent among us have to admit that even in the liberal West there are limits to humour on the grounds of good taste and offence – would a joke about the Holocaust be considered acceptable, for example?

'I think the big problem this country has is being politically correct... I don't frankly have time for total political correctness.'
– **Donald Trump (b. 1946)**

₀010 GOING BEGGING

Linda works in a lavish office building in the city. Her clerical job is less impressive than the office's marble lobby might suggest, but she counts herself among the fortunate, as she has a job, her own flat, and a disposable income. Every day when she walks out of the underground station, she passes several people begging. She will usually spare a pound or whatever change she has to one person each weekday. She doesn't choose at random, but has her favourites. She tends to go for the people she sees regularly in the same spot rather than the newcomers. There is the woman who is surrounded by shopping bags

BEGGARS ARE A DAILY PRESENCE ON THE STREETS IN MANY CITIES. BUT IS GIVING A FEW POUNDS TO BEGGARS TO ASSUAGE OUR GUILT THE MOST EFFECTIVE WAY WE COULD BE HELPING THEM?

stuffed with old clothes; she mutters to herself, but thanks Linda effusively when she drops some change in her lap. There is also an old man who always nods at her in greeting, whether she gives him something or not.

She is less likely to give to the younger men and women that congregate outside the station: the ravaged-looking junkies, who look like they might make a grab for her bag if she got too close, or the dirty man who always has a bottle of something on the go and often shouts obscenities at passers-by. Today, though, there is a new face, a young man with a dog curled at his feet. The dog, who looks as though he could do with a good meal, reminds her of her own childhood dog, and though the man is not one of her 'regulars', she picks him for the day's donation.

Beggars' Opera

We learned in the 'latte' dilemma earlier that Peter Singer advocates giving to the poor. However, he advocates 'effective altruism', that is, choosing the best way of alleviating poverty. Linda's heart is in the right place when she gives money to people who are clearly less well-off than she is. But how effective are her donations?

She picks people who are familiar and whom she finds unthreatening, or those whom she feels sorry for, but are they the most deserving of her help? She avoids giving to people she assumes to be drug users, thinking that they would use her money to feed their addiction, but she doesn't know how people use the money she gives them. Even if they do use the money to sustain themselves, the life expectancy of someone living on the streets is some thirty years shorter than the average lifespan. So by giving money to beggars, Linda may be encouraging them to remain in a lifestyle that will result in their early deaths. Also, her donations are based on personal criteria rather than trying to decide how the money she gives would be most effectively spent to alleviate poverty. Would it be preferable for Linda to donate the money to local charities that work with those sleeping rough, or to campaigning groups that work to end homelessness – in other words, attempt to enact the 'effective altruism' advocated by Singer?

011 A DISCRIMINATING EYE

Morgan is a man of the old school. He has worked for the firm for thirty years – was hired by the boss himself. The old boss is straight as a die, speaks his mind and doesn't care who you are or where you come from as long as you can put in a hard day's work. He doesn't have a son to take over the business when he dies, but his daughter is now running the show.

Morgan looks through the pile of papers on his desk. They are the CVs of the latest batch of applicants for the firm, but she's insisted that they be 'anonymised' – no names, ages, sexes (though she said 'genders'). When she handed him the CVs, he asked how he was supposed to figure out who would be any good and who would fit in at the office. 'You've got all the information you need', she stated. 'Just go by their qualifications and past experience and pick the best people for the vacancies we have.' 'But', he'd said, 'What if I pick a girl for the loading bay? And what about the packers? What if I pick a boy?' She didn't seem to understand. After that, he hadn't even dared bring up the issue of age, religion and race. This was an old-fashioned firm, with old-fashioned ways of doing things. What would the guys say if the new loader he hired was a girl or a Muslim? Or the girls, if they got some school kid as a packer?

Sticks and stones ...

Political correctness began with the banning of certain words that had historically been used to describe different social and ethnic groups, women and sexual minorities, but are now deemed to be derogatory, offensive and discriminatory. But political correctness has moved on from the banning of certain words and expressions to establishing limits as to what an individual is required to reveal about themselves in certain situations, when being of a certain marital status, age, gender, religion, race or ethnic background might put them at a disadvantage. Hence Morgan's problem, as he is deprived of information that he would have used to distinguish between different candidates.

Words as loud as actions

British philosopher of language John L. Austin (1911–60) came up with the idea of 'speech acts' and 'performative utterances', which he explained rather simply as: 'By saying something, we do something'. Austin's work was purely concerned with language, but later writers have used the concepts he developed to show how they are used to create social categories. American philosopher and gender theorist Judith Butler (b. 1956) has used Austin's theory of performative utterances to claim that words are not inherently derogatory but only contextually, thus undermining the idea of political correctness.

POLITICAL CORRECTNESS IS NO LONGER JUST ABOUT WORDS THAT DENIGRATE, DISEMPOWER AND DIVIDE. IT IS ALSO ABOUT THE ASSUMPTIONS WE MAKE ON THE BASIS OF GENDER, RACE, AGE OR RELIGION. HOW MUCH DOES AN EMPLOYER NEED TO KNOW ABOUT A PROSPECTIVE EMPLOYEE?

The N-word

The man says, 'And then this N-word walks into the bar...' Your reaction to the use of the N-word primarily depends on who is saying it, who is listening and what the context is. Context one: Comedian Chris Rock is doing standup at a comedy club in front of a sophisticated metropolitan audience, who understand how he is using the word. While it is possible for a person of black heritage to have internalised racist attitudes, it is not very likely in the case of Chris Rock or the many rap and hip-hop artists who use the N-word in their lyrics. Context two: Two close friends greet each other with the N-word. Is it OK only when they are both black? Or could a white person get away with using it in this situation?

The G-word

There is no well-used equivalent term for white people in the Western world. And though it might be a good idea to try and invent one, the power of the N-word derives from its association with the history of slavery and racial discrimination in the US. One term that might be considered derogatory for white people is the Chinese word *gweilo*, which is used to describe foreigners in China. The word means 'ghost man' or 'devil man'. It is not always used pejoratively, but depending on the intention of the speaker and the context, it could certainly be used in a racist way, and only a native or fluent speaker of Chinese would be exactly sure of the intended meaning upon hearing it.

012 RESOURCE POVERTY

Aaron and his wife and children are realising a long-held dream of visiting Yosemite National Park, in California. They have loaded up the car and driven across two states to reach the park. Aaron remembers how, years ago, his father had taken him hiking in the park. Then, gazing on the expansive vistas and empty trails, Aaron had felt transported back to the days of the pioneers. During the drive he has been telling his own boys about the vast, empty wilderness, but as they reach the access road to the park, they pull into a huge traffic jam. It seems that a lot of other families have also picked this holiday weekend to visit the park. Everything is jam-packed, and even when they finally get into the park, there seem to be people everywhere.

WE LIVE IN A WORLD OF FINITE NATURAL RESOURCES BUT WITH A POPULATION THAT CONTINUES TO GROW EXPONENTIALLY. WITH ONLY SO MUCH TO GO AROUND, HOW SHOULD WE ALLOCATE OUR LIMITED RESOURCES?

The tragedy of the commons

Originally used to illustrate the problem of overgrazing on public land, the tragedy of the commons was applied by American philosopher Garrett Hardin (1915–2003) to all the Earth's natural resources on which we all depend for survival. Hardin argued the case for some form of population control in order to maintain reasonable standards of living (or at least ensure survival, in the worst-case scenario). But were we to follow this course of action, how would we decide who should be allowed to reproduce? And how would we allocate the Earth's remaining resources?

013 **LEVEL PLAYING FIELD**

Mathilda is firm: Her eldest daughter Lauri is not going to 'cheat' her way into university by making use of its affirmative-action programme. Doesn't the girl realise that if she wants to amount to anything, she'll have to work for it? Mathilda was the first woman in her family to go to university. And she got in on her own merits. There had been no 'affirmative action' programmes when she had battled poverty, low expectations, prejudice and discrimination, but she had overcome it all, and graduated top of her class, which had put quite a few noses out of joint.

'But, Mum', Lauri whines, 'it's a really good university, and they're making it easy for people like me to get in.' 'People like you!' Mathilda explodes. 'There is no "people like you", or like them; there's just people!' Lauri rolls her eyes, gets up from the table and goes to her room. 'You are too hard on the girl', her husband, Joe, starts. 'She's right; going there will open doors for her. And once she's in, she'll have to work as hard as anyone else to pass her exams.'

'The trouble is', Mathilda thinks, 'I'm right, but so are they.' The name of that university on her daughter's CV would open a lot of doors, but it also feels like cheating or, even worse, an admission that Lauri doesn't think she's good enough to compete with the others on equal terms. This was never meant for a girl like Lauri, whose parents both went to university, who went to a good school, and was encouraged and expected to excel. She would be taking the place of a boy or girl who really needs the step-up.

Affirm or discriminate?

The main argument deployed by the American philosopher George Sher (b. 1942) against affirmative action is that, by shifting the eligibility criteria from people's ability to their membership of a particular social group, it devalues their subsequent achievements. Another common criticism is that it acts as a form of reverse discrimination, unfairly disadvantaging people who might be just as able, but who are passed over because they belong to the wrong social group. Some critics also argue that though it was needed in the 'bad old days', affirmative action is now no longer necessary. Supporters counter that discrimination, deprivation and exclusion continue to limit the opportunities of many.

INEQUALITY OF OPPORTUNITY SEEMS TO BE A FACT OF LIFE FOR SOME PEOPLE. BUT BY GIVING CERTAIN GROUPS A HELPING HAND, DO WE END UP CREATING NEW KINDS OF UNFAIRNESS?

'If you don't like affirmative action, what is your plan to guarantee a level playing field of opportunity?'
– **Maynard Jackson (1938–2003)**

014 WASTE NOT, WANT NOT

It is Amy's first day volunteering at the local charity shop. She is in the backroom where donations are examined, sorted and priced before being put on sale. Suzanne, the shop manager, explains the process. There is a mountain of bags to be sorted into four large storage bins. Anything expensive or with a designer label goes into Bin One. Bin Two is for mid-range clothing, and Bin Thee is for the polyester tracksuits and the garish or drab. The waste bin is for anything soiled or damaged, and the rejects from Bin Three.

Amy looks at the huge pile of bags. 'I never knew we got so much! How are we ever going to sell it all?' she asks. 'Oh, we haven't the room for most of this stuff', Suzanne replies. 'I go through Bins One and Two and pick

EVERY YEAR, MILLIONS OF POUNDS' WORTH OF GOODS ARE DONATED TO CHARITY SHOPS. SOME ARE RE-SOLD IN THE DEVELOPING WORLD. IS IT RIGHT THAT THESE CHARITABLE GIFTS END UP MAKING SOMEONE ELSE A PROFIT?

the clothes for the shop, but most of it goes to a wholesaler.' 'And what do they do with it?' Amy asks. 'The stuff from Bin One goes to vintage shops here and overseas', Suzanne explains, throwing a ripped T-shirt into the waste bin. 'Bins Two and Three are sold in different parts of the developing world, and the waste bin gets shredded and made into all kinds of stuff.' Amy looks so surprised that Suzanne goes on, 'It would take years to sell all this stuff, so the charity gets the cash. The clothes are reused or recycled, and some of the people who made the clothes in the first place get a chance to wear them'.

Making waste pay

The recycling business is a multi-billion-pound industry. In the 'developed world' societies of conspicuous wasters are fast becoming conspicuous recyclers, recycling not just plastic, tin cans, paper and glass, but clothing, electronics, car parts – anything that has been made has a value to someone somewhere in the world. Amy is concerned that the clothing donations people make are sold to commercial wholesalers, who sell them on to consumers in the developing world. But she doesn't worry about the recyclable rubbish that the city sells to recyclers, and that ends up back in the shops as new products. For the charities, it's a win-win situation, and the clothes have an extended life, rather than rotting in warehouses or going to landfill.

'My company in the US, Pratt Industries USA, has grown from scratch to become a billion-dollar business based on recycling.'
– **Anthony Pratt**

⟋015 HIGH ROLLERS

Two friends, Rob, an American, and his British friend James, are in Rob's backyard having a barbecue. Their kids are playing a mix of cricket and baseball, and their wives are bringing out the slaw and salads from the kitchen. As they throw sausages onto the grill, James tells Rob about an item he saw on last night's news.

'Do you know how much the highest paid CEO earns in this country?' he asks. 'I don't know', Rob replies, 'forty, fifty mil?' '$143,077,442!' exclaims James. Even Rob is willing to concede that this is a lot of cash, and more than ten times what he earns, but he also admires the guy. 'That's the American dream', he explains. 'But is it?' James asks. 'Isn't the American dream about everyone having the same chance to make it rich? I bet that that guy didn't make it from the shop floor to the boardroom.'

THE DIFFERENCE BETWEEN WHAT THE HIGHEST AND LOWEST EARNERS ARE PAID HAS NEVER BEEN GREATER. IS THERE A POINT AT WHICH SOMEONE CAN BE SAID TO EARN TOO MUCH MONEY?

The sports-star analogy

According to Oxfam, the world's richest one percent own more than the remaining 99 percent put together. We might ask how many houses, Learjets and cars one person can really use – but these are not criteria that are used to justify wealth in our current economic system.

Forty years ago, American libertarian philosopher Robert Nozick (1938–2002) justified differences in pay, or wage differentials (which were much lower at the time), by drawing an analogy with the earnings of sports stars. Then, the highest-paid American sportsperson earned $77.2 million in salary ($23.2 million) and endorsements ($54 million). Leaving the endorsements to one side and looking just at his salary, Nozick asked his readers to consider how many fans the sportsman had worldwide, and how many of them would be more than happy to pay one or two dollars to watch him play.

His argument doesn't carry over that smoothly to CEOs, but if one looks at the number of employees of a corporation, as well as the employees of other firms that are dependent on it, it is possible to arrive at a per capita value of the CEO. This could justify the salary for a successful boss of a major corporation, but what about the salaries of heads of firms that are laying off workers? Or those who have few employees and make money through investments?

'We cannot continue to allow hundreds of millions of people to go hungry while resources that could be used to help them are sucked up by those at the top.'
– **Winnie Byanima**

⌀016 READ ALL ABOUT IT

'That poor child!' Lynn exclaims, putting the paper down on the kitchen table. Her partner David looks up from his own paper and reads the headline, 'Manhunt on for Kidnapper Dad', splashed across the front page. He'd seen the story on the news the night before. According to the report he had half-watched, the father had been denied any visitation rights by the child's mother and her new girlfriend. David is a bit hazy on the details, but the anchor had said that the case was about upholding American 'family values' as well as the rights of the father, and doing 'what was best for the child'.

When David tries to argue the father's case, Lynn dismisses him, saying, 'Oh, that is so much like a man – boys sticking together'. According to Lynn's account, the story is not as simple as he first thought. The father had made a private arrangement with the same-sex couple (donating sperm so that they could have a child), but when the boy had turned four he had decided that he wanted a greater hand in his son's upbringing, even though that had never been part of the original deal.

BY CONSULTING TWO DIFFERENT NEWS OUTLETS, WE MAY GET A COMPLETELY DIFFERENT VIEW OF THE SAME EVENT. IS BIAS NECESSARILY BUILT INTO THE MEDIA, OR SHOULD WE BE ABLE TO EXPECT SOME KIND OF BALANCE AND OBJECTIVITY?

David turns to the news pages of his own paper, which carries the same story under the headline, 'Desperate dad hounded across two states'. It claims that there had been an unspoken understanding between the biological parents, and it was pressure from the mother's wife that had caused the rift. The article almost makes her out to be a home-wrecker who broke up a happy heterosexual couple.

Left and right

According to the economist Timothy Groseclose (b. 1964), the US media has a significant left-leaning bias, which, if removed, would always lead the country to vote like the solid Republican states of Texas and Kentucky. Other commentators, including conservative journalist Andrew Sullivan (b. 1963), have asserted the opposite case. They cannot both be right, so does that mean that there exists some kind of balance in the US media, or are other factors at play when people are polled about the issue? In the case of David and Lynn in the example above, in addition to the bias in the news outlets they consult, are the couple already biased by their respective genders and therefore more likely to be sympathetic to either the mother or the father?

Thought experiment: *The Daily Planet*

According to Groseclose, when most people think of the media, they think of Superman's fictional newspaper the *Daily Planet*, where Clark Kent and Lois Lane work, and where the straight-talking editor, Perry White, decides the stories they cover. The reality, Groseclose says, is that journalists are much more independent when it comes to deciding which stories to cover and how to present them, and are thus able to bias the reporting of what are usually seen as conservative news outlets. However, given that the choice of stories is an important factor in deciding the news agenda of a particular outlet, how likely is it that a liberal journalist would really last long working for a conservative organisation?

POLITICAL

'Democracy is the worst form of government, except for all the others.'
— Winston Churchill (1874–1965)

🌀 017 THE TORTURER'S APPRENTICE

Mine's a funny old job. Five years' training in all of the relevant aspects of psychology, physiology, anaesthetics, international politics, current affairs and applied ethics, all on top of my initial medical degree. And, chances are, when it's all done, and I finally qualify, I'll never be needed.

Only if the worst happens – only if we get a genuine real-life 'ticking bomb scenario' – will I be called upon to actually *do* what I have been trained to do. Of course, it's a job I couldn't have even contemplated doing in the old days: the days of thumbscrews, racks and pincers. I wouldn't have the stomach for any of *that* – nor waterboarding. But now it's all completely civilised and above-board. The chamber is clean and sanitary, even comfortable. There are clean sheets, soft pillows, the lot. There are medical and psychological checks beforehand and the subject is monitored throughout. They are even offered post-trauma counselling afterwards. There is no blood, no bruising, no broken bones – no physical damage of any kind. Just a quick whiff of a paralysing drug and then a psychotropic drug. No writhing. No moaning and screaming. No unpleasantness of any sort.

A PERSON WHO WANTS TO KILL, MAIM AND DESTROY SUFFERS A FEW MINUTES' AGONY, AND THOUSANDS OF INNOCENT LIVES ARE SAVED. AND IT IS ALL DONE IN THE MOST HUMANE MANNER POSSIBLE. SURELY NO ONE COULD OBJECT. COULD THEY?

Of course, that psychotropic thing's no picnic. I had to experience it as part of my training (at a mere fraction of the actual dose). And believe you me, that's one experience I never want to repeat. The terrorist won't want to repeat it either; that's been clinically proven. So rather than face another dose, he or she will tell us everything we need to know – guaranteed. Thousands, perhaps millions, of lives are saved. Unpleasant political and social repercussions are avoided. The terrorist is saved from him – or herself. Everyone's a winner.

The ticking bomb scenario

Most people think that torture is unethical. But does that mean its use could never be justified?

The ticking bomb scenario is a thought experiment designed to confront people with that question. It runs as follows:

A terrorist group has concealed a nuclear bomb in a major city. The group's leader has been apprehended by the authorities. He admits that he knows the whereabouts of the device, but refuses to reveal its location. The authorities have developed an infallible method of torture.

- Would it be unethical to use it?
- Would it be unethical not to use it?
- Is this a case where there is no ethically acceptable course of action?
- In which case, isn't the use of torture – arguably the lesser of the two evils – justified?

The case against torture

Here are some arguments against using torture. How many of them have been addressed in the account of the torturer's apprentice?

- It is illegal under international law.
- The physical and psychological damage it causes is often permanent.
- It is counterproductive. You may get some useful information in the short term, but you damage your country's reputation – and encourage further acts of terrorism – in the long term.
- Intelligence extracted by torture is unreliable. Victims will say anything to make the torture stop.
- If you allow torture in special cases, for example in ticking bomb scenarios, you normalise torture.

018 HANDS ACROSS THE SEA

Remember Sally, whom we met at the beginning of Dilemma 2? She agonised over whether she should continue to buy her daily treat – the latte she bought every night on her way home from work – after she had been told by a charity collector that for the price of her milky coffee she could save a person's sight. Now imagine that Sally is a senior member of a national government with special responsibility for international aid. She doesn't just have a few pounds to hand out that would change the life of one person, but hundreds of millions of pounds that could change the lives of thousands of people in whole regions and countries.

Sally, however, is no expert in international development; nor is she an academic specialising in ethics. She is an elected politician. Nevertheless, Sally is truly committed to finding the best way to distribute the aid at her disposal,

EVERY YEAR BILLIONS OF DOLLARS, POUNDS AND EUROS ARE DONATED IN INTERNATIONAL AID TO DEVELOPING COUNTRIES, BUT WHAT CRITERIA SHOULD DECIDE WHO RECEIVES AID AND, BY IMPLICATION, WHO DOES NOT?

without favouring her country's allies, or maximising the aid's commercial or political potential. So what criteria should she base her decisions on? She could opt for objective measures such as income and spending power, but these exclude so much; or she could aim to 'maximise individual happiness', but happiness is a rather fuzzy concept that is difficult to pin down. She needs to find an approach that can combine both objective and subjective measures.

The capability approach

In order to decide who is most deserving of aid, Sally could use the 'capability approach', first outlined by Indian economist and philosopher Amartya Kumar Sen (b. 1933) and elaborated by Martha Nussbaum (b. 1947), professor of law and ethics at the University of Chicago. This would enable her to evaluate the life chances of different people, while taking into account their cultural diversity. The approach uses two basic concepts: 'functionings' and 'capabilities'. Functionings are the things a person can be or do, such as being well fed or malnourished, and being able to vote or take drugs; capabilities are a person's real abilities or freedoms to do these things. Functionings are morally neutral: they can be good, bad or nuanced and context-dependent. The act of travelling is a functioning, which in theory all humans have, but a person's capability to travel is the ability to travel freely without being impeded by factors outside of one's control, which may be limited by a lack of means, or by social or political constraints.

Hunger games

Sen cites the example of hunger to illustrate how two people can participate in the same 'functioning', but with radically different capabilities. The first person is hungry because he is starving for lack of food because he is too poor to buy any, while the second person is hungry because she is fasting for religious reasons, and thus has chosen to go hungry.

♂019 FAIR DEVELOPMENT

Imagine a town called Everytown. In Northside are the grandest houses. That's also where most of the town's main amenities are: the bank, the mall, the park, the town hall, the hospital, the best school, the health club and the golf course. Immediately to the south is Middleside, an area of middle-sized houses, comfortable but not flashy. They are close enough to the town's amenities to benefit from them, though less so than their northern neighbours.

The most southerly part of town, Southside, is a rundown slum. The houses are small and mean, most of the shops are boarded up, and the public amenities are almost non-existent. Southsiders are too far from the richer part of town to benefit from its civic amenities, even if they were welcomed there, which they are usually not. If someone from Southside strays into Northside, they are made to feel distinctly unwelcome by the locals.

THE WORLD IS SPLIT AMONG THE HAVES, MAINLY IN THE GLOBAL NORTH, AND THE HAVE-NOTS, MAINLY IN THE GLOBAL SOUTH. CAN WE REBALANCE THE WORLD ECONOMY THROUGH DEVELOPMENT?

Now imagine that you have just been elected mayor of Everytown, with the backing of the residents of Middleside and Southside, and with a mandate to improve their areas and make the whole of Everytown a better place to live. You have the resources of city hall at your disposal, and whatever loans you can raise from the rather conservative Everytown Bank. You need to divert resources from Northside so that you can use them to develop Southside, but the city newspaper, radio and TV, all owned by Northside residents, are already accusing you of being a socialist, if not a communist. How do you persuade Northsiders to back your plan to improve the lot of Southsiders?

Life, liberty and the pursuit of happiness

During the latter half of the twentieth century, after the dismantling of the great colonial empires, the most pressing concern was the social, political and economic development of what was then known as the Third World (Africa, the Near East, South and Central America and South and Southeast Asia), and how the First World (Europe and North America) should make up for centuries of exploitation.

The issue prompted American human development theorist Denis Goulet (1931–2006) to create the field of developmental ethics, which examined development not just from the point of view of the immediate needs of people in the poorer parts of the world for food, healthcare and shelter, but also included the idea of equity between the world's richest and poorest, and outlined the basic human rights that every human being should take as their due.

The question Goulet asked in 1971, 'How can moral guidelines influence decisions of those who hold power?' remains unresolved, and has now been made even more difficult to answer because of the problems of pollution and climate change and how they affect the sustainability of development. Goulet's work led to Amartya Sen and Martha Nussbaum's Capabilities Approach (see pp. 48–49), which remains the ethical basis for the world's major development and international aid programmes.

WHO SHOULD GET IN?

MIGRATION HAS BECOME THE NUMBER ONE GEOPOLITICAL ISSUE IN THE WORLD TODAY, WITH VAST FLOWS OF REFUGEES AND ASYLUM SEEKERS DISPLACED BY WAR AND POLITICAL OPPRESSION, AND LEGAL AND ILLEGAL MIGRANTS WHO WANT TO IMPROVE THEIR ECONOMIC OPPORTUNITIES. NO TWO COUNTRIES ON THE PLANET SEEM TO OPERATE THE SAME CRITERIA FOR GRANTING CITIZENSHIP OR CONTROLLING IMMIGRATION. IS A REAL OPEN-BORDERS POLICY POSSIBLE OR JUST AN IMPOSSIBLE DREAM?

Imagine you are in charge of your country's borders for a day, and you have the power to decide who gets in and who does not. Five people present themselves at your office to make their cases for admission. Even if a person has a legal right of entry, is it right to let them in?

020 THE CITIZEN

The first person to apply for entry to your country is a citizen, with a passport to prove it. The passport checks out, but you are surprised that she needs to talk to you through an interpreter. You discover that she is a citizen because she was born while transiting through an airport in your country, and the law stipulates that anyone born in the country is automatically a citizen. Legally, she has every right to admission, but is that enough for you to grant her entry with all the rights and privileges that go with it? You could argue that she acquired her citizenship by sheer luck: being born during a layover between flights. But what about other citizens, including yourself? In a sense, being born in one country rather than another is always a question of luck, depending on where your parents chose to be at the time of your birth.

021 THE LEGAL MIGRANT

The second person to present himself at your border post identifies himself as a legal migrant who has been granted a passport after completing the necessary years of residency required for citizenship. Enquiring further, you discover that he holds a second passport – that of his homeland – as neither country insists that a person can hold only one citizenship at any time. Again, according to the law, as a passport holder, he has the legal right to enter the country. The situation is complicated in your mind, however, because his country of origin is currently not on good terms with your own. What if the man has divided loyalties? If a conflict developed between the two countries concerned, what would his status as a citizen be then?

⁰⁄₀022 THE ILLEGAL MIGRANT

On the face of it, the third person to come to see you seems to be a much more clear-cut case: She admits to being an illegal immigrant. You are about to stamp 'refused admission' on her passport, when she pleads extenuating circumstances. She was trafficked into the country to be a sex worker when she was still a teenager, but managed to escape her captors with the help of a young man who was himself an illegal immigrant. That was twenty years ago. Since then, the couple have made a life together in the country. They have a family of three children who, by being born in the country, are automatically citizens. The children are still at school, and if their parents were deported they would not be able to follow them, as they only hold one passport. They would then be alone, and would need to be looked after by the state at considerable expense, until they reached adulthood. By deporting the woman in this case, you would not only break up a family, but you would put an added strain on the already stretched social security system.

⁰⁄₀023 THE REFUGEE

The fourth person to walk into your office is an eighteen-year-old refugee from a distant war zone. He managed to smuggle himself into the country aboard a commercial vehicle and was only discovered after he had crossed the border. Again, his case seems as if it might be easier to resolve. But again there are mitigating circumstances. First, you are aware that his home country is a war zone, so it would be impossible to return him safely. Second, he has told you that he is an orphan, as his close family have been killed.

024 THE ASYLUM SEEKER

The final person who presents himself to you immediately claims political asylum in your country, stating that if he were returned to his own country, he would be arrested, detained without trial, tortured and probably executed. You know that the country he comes from has a repressive dictatorship, which routinely arrests and detains its citizens without due process, and is rumoured to eliminate political opponents. Before reaching your country, however, the man has passed through several other states where he could and should have claimed political asylum but chose not to. When you ask him about this, he explains that the other countries were not welcoming of or safe for asylum seekers from his own country. You could attempt to return him to the previous state he transited through, but that country might either refuse him entry, or worse, deport him back to his homeland.

Living in the Middle Ages

Philosopher and political scientist Joseph Carens (b. 1945) compares the restrictions on immigration in the modern world to medieval feudalism. In feudal society, status was inherited: If you were born into the nobility, you were privileged from birth, and if you were born into the peasantry, you were disadvantaged from birth. Today, if you are lucky enough to be born in the developed world, it is as though you are a member of the feudal nobility, with greatly enhanced life chances, and if you are born in the developing world, it is as though you are a medieval peasant, with greatly reduced life chances. This injustice is maintained by restrictions on the free movement of peoples across national borders, which determine people's opportunities in life not by ability, but by an accident of birth. But is a world with truly open borders nothing more than a utopian pipe dream?

♋ 025 CLOSED MINDS

Karim is a third-year politics student at an Ivy League university who is spending a term at a similarly prestigious British university. One evening in the student common room, he sees a poster for a lecture by an Islamic cleric on how to lead an Islamic life in a secular Western context. His own family (second-generation Lebanese Americans) are not particularly religious, though they keep some of the cultural traditions of their homeland (in the lax way that most secular Westerners from Christian backgrounds pay lip service to Christmas or Easter). He has heard of this particular imam, who is said to be something of a firebrand, and he is curious to hear him speak, and if necessary, to challenge his views.

The day of the lecture arrives and Karim goes to the lecture theatre in good time to get a front row seat, but when he gets there he is surprised to see a group of demonstrators outside. Several of them are brandishing placards in English and Arabic, seemingly both for and against the cleric, and there are security guards guarding the closed doors. When he asks a bystander what is going on, the student replies, 'It's outrageous censorship! He's been no-platformed.'

The 'no platform' rule that the bystander is referring to is the British National Union of Students policy of banning people that hold certain controversial points of view from speaking at universities. Karim's university has conceded, for fear of a disturbance should the cleric be allowed to speak. Its complaint, apart from the conservative attitudes of the cleric concerned, is that the audience attending the lecture was to be segregated on gender lines, with women and men sitting in separate sections.

The closing of minds

The American philosopher and classicist Allan Bloom (1930–1992) addressed the issue of political correctness at US universities in *The Closing of the American Mind* (1987). In the book Bloom objects to the spoon-feeding of politically correct opinions in American universities, which, he says, stifles intellectual debate and accomplishment. Bloom does not deal directly with the kind of no-platform policy that Karim experiences while in the UK, but he would no doubt be opposed to the kind of censorship that this silencing of certain viewpoints entails.

DO STUDENTS NEED TO BE PROTECTED FROM VIEWS THAT MIGHT OFFEND OR RADICALISE THEM, OR SHOULD UNIVERSITIES BE PLACES WHERE NON-MAINSTREAM IDEAS CAN BE DISCUSSED AND CHALLENGED?

'I disapprove of what you say, but I will defend to the death your right to say it.'
– Attributed to Voltaire (1694–1778) but actually written by Evelyn Hall (1868–1956) as an illustration of Voltaire's beliefs

⸓026 IN THE DRIVING SEAT

Marshall does not believe that dogs should be kept as pets. In the next elections, he stands for the ADA (Anti-Dog Alliance), a party that advocates the banning of all pet dogs, on the grounds of animal cruelty, waste of resources that might be used for humans, and hygiene, because dogs foul the parks and pavements. He is elected in his district, as are about ten others in the party nationwide. It is a small party and would almost be insignificant – were it not for the fact that the majority party is short of ten votes for an absolute majority. On behalf of the ADA, Marshall agrees to join the government, but only on the condition that the government begins to implement its main policy of banning pet dogs.

The leader of the majority party agrees, but when it comes to announcing the government's policies, they fall very short of an overall ban. He offers some measures: banning dogs from parks, high fines or even prison terms for people who allow their dogs to foul the pavements, and a limit on how many dogs one person can own. He explains to Marshall that an outright ban would be difficult if not impossible to implement, that there might be riots by dog owners, and that a slow implementation of the policy – perhaps over twenty years – through education and persuasion, would have a much better chance of success.

Marshall has two options:

• He can refuse to join the government, forcing it to look to form a coalition with other parties, many of which, though individually smaller, are vehemently pro-dog.

• He can join the government on the grounds that at least he will gain some anti-dog measures, with a promise of a total ban in future – however distant (and unlikely).

If he does agree, however, he will be betraying his constituents, and is unlikely to get re-elected next time round.

The coach-driver theory of democracy

French political writer Paul Louis Courier (1772–1825) lived through the most turbulent phases of French political history: the French Revolution of 1789, the First French Empire (1804–1815), and the restoration of the monarchy (1814–1830) – governments with very different approaches to democracy. His preferred analogy for democracy was the coach-driver theory, which defines the head of the government as a figure with no authority. While everyone admits that democracy is based on popular sovereignty, it is not enough of a guarantee that people have the right to disobey, but by saying the government has no more power than a hired coach driver – or a chauffeur, to modernise the analogy – we are in no doubt as to who is supposedly in charge. Although many democratic leaders act as though they are in charge of the coach (or limo) of state, should they not be merely instruments, whose only function is to implement the wishes of the people who elect them?

REPRESENTATIVE DEMOCRACY HAS MANY PARADOXES BUILT IN. IN THEORY, ELECTED OFFICIALS ARE SUPPOSED TO CARRY OUT THE WISHES OF THE VOTERS THEY REPRESENT, BUT THEY RARELY DO. IS THERE A SYSTEM THAT WOULD SERVE US BETTER?

⚙ 027 TAXING MATTERS

Sarah is reading a news story about major US corporations that register their profits offshore, so that they pay little or no tax. One of the firms named and shamed is the coffee chain that she visits for her daily caffeine fix.

Sarah pays her taxes – she has no choice. She has no money to pay accountants and tax lawyers to hide her meagre income in Panama or some other tax haven. She doesn't agree with everything that the taxes are spent on, but then who does? She thinks it probably all evens out in the end, and what choice does she really have? She doesn't currently use all the services the state provides – schools or old peoples' homes, for example – she has no children, but she may in the future, and she will get old. She resents the fact that the coffee chain avoids paying taxes. After all, they depend on the transit and social infrastructure for their staff, and they reap vast profits from local citizens. Don't they have a duty to put something back into the community?

'There is no moral obligation to pay a homeless person who does an inferior job of washing your windshield without your permission while you are stuck at a stop light. Why should there be a moral obligation to pay government for providing some inferior service that you do not want and did not ask for?'

– Robert McGee (b. 1947)

Master and servant

Similar to Courier's coach-driver theory of democracy, Italian Dominican theologians Daniello Concina (1687–1756) and Giovanni Patuzzi (1700–1769) argued that the state can be likened to a servant, and that as the employers, the citizens owe a 'stipend' to their employee, 'just as a servant's wage, is due in strict justice'. Paying taxes is therefore not only a duty, it is just and fair.

BIG CORPORATIONS AND RICH INDIVIDUALS THAT AVOID PAYING TAX ARE SLAMMED AS UNPATRIOTIC AND IMMORAL, BUT DO THEY HAVE A CASE TO MAKE AGAINST PAYING TAXES?

No taxation without appreciation

Several centuries later, economist Robert McGee would beg to differ. In *The Ethics of Tax Evasion*, he justifies tax avoidance in the following situations:

- when the government is corrupt or commits human rights abuses
- when the citizens are unable to pay
- when the tax system is unfair
- when taxes pay for things that do not benefit the taxpayer
- when taxes fund an unpopular war
- because of religious, moral or philosophical objections.

The most striking example of unjust taxation that he cites, is that of the Jews in Nazi Germany, who were forced to pay taxes to fund their own extermination.

028 A DOG-EAT-DOG WORLD

Marshall (see pp. 58–59), now head of the ADA (Anti-Dog Alliance), is representing his country at an international conference on dogs. A few years in office have tempered his initial zeal to achieve his aim of ridding the country of all pet dogs – his party's platform. As he is a minority partner in the administration, all he has achieved so far are token measures, such as banning dogs from certain public spaces and limiting the number of dogs any one person can own. But these small steps have not made much of a dent in the country's dog population, and even these measures are constantly being challenged in the courts.

His constituents are becoming restless. With elections next year, he has to pull something big out of the hat, or he'll be looking for a new job. At the conference the representative of country A approaches him privately, inviting him to a secret meeting. Country A is willing to take as many dogs as Marshall can ship to them. 'What would you do with them?' Marshall asks. 'Let's say that our population', the foreign envoy replies, 'have different tastes than yours'. Marshall is at first horrified, but then urges himself to be realistic. We could say the dogs are being rehomed overseas, he thinks. They will certainly be well fed. And no one back home need be any the wiser.

Country A is considered a hostile power, but Marshall has an answer for that, too. The dog-rehoming initiative could be painted as a breakthrough in international relations.

'It is not love, or morality, or international law that determines the outcome of world affairs, but the changing distribution of organised force.'
– William Woodruff (1916–2008)

Politics in the real world

Niccolò Machiavelli (1469–1527), author of *The Prince* (1513), and Chancellor Otto von Bismarck (1815–1898), first unifier of Germany, would have praised Marshall's keen understanding of *Realpolitik* (from the German for 'practical' or 'actual' politics). Bismarck observed wryly that, 'People never lie so much as after a hunt, during a war or before an election'. He would have echoed the following criticisms of political ethics:

- The basis of politics is a no-holds-barred competition for power and advantage between individuals and states. In international politics in particular, politicians cannot be bound by ethical considerations, as this would handicap them against their rivals.
- Another criticism is that ethics focuses too much on specific policies that obscure the true causes of political and social injustice.

DO ETHICS HAVE ANY PLACE IN REAL-WORLD POLITICS? SOME WOULD ARGUE THAT THEY DON'T, ESPECIALLY IN THE FIELD OF INTERNATIONAL RELATIONS, WHERE ONE'S RIVALS MAY BE WORKING WITH DIFFERENT ETHICS — OR NO ETHICS AT ALL.

LAW AND ORDER

'Law and order exist for the purpose of establishing justice and when they fail in this purpose they become the dangerously structured dams that block the flow of social progress.'
– **Martin Luther King Jr (1929–1968)**

ℬ029 JUST ANOTHER BAR FIGHT

Paul has always been quick-tempered. Especially when he's had a few drinks. One evening he was drinking in a crowded pub when he exchanged heated words with Max over whose turn it was to be served. Max refused to back down. Paul became angrier and angrier, and eventually lashed out, punching Max squarely on the jaw. Max dropped like a stone, hitting his head on the edge of the bar as he fell. He was dead before he reached the ground. He left behind a widow and two children. It was not the first time that Paul had got into a fight. So, at his trial, the judge sentenced him to fifteen years.

In another town, Harry – a man very much like Paul – got into a bar fight in similar circumstances. He, too, landed a punch squarely on the jaw of his antagonist, Jeff. Jeff fell to the ground too, but luckily he suffered nothing worse than a broken tooth. It was the first time that Harry had got into a fight. So, at his trial, the judge sentences him to twelve hours' community service and ordered him to pay Jeff's dental bills.

YOU ARE A SENIOR JUDGE WHO HAS BEEN ASKED TO REVIEW THE SENTENCING IN THESE TWO CASES. DO YOU THINK THE SENTENCES ARE FAIR? IS IT RIGHT THAT PAUL SHOULD RECEIVE A HARSHER SENTENCE THAN HARRY?

Thinking it through

So far as we can tell, is Paul any worse a person than Harry? No. They both lost their tempers and lashed out with their fists.

Was Paul's behaviour towards Max any worse than Harry's behaviour towards Jeff? Again, no. They behaved equally badly.

So is Paul any more morally culpable than Harry? Surely not. How can we judge two people differently for doing the very same thing?

In that case, why should Paul be punished more severely than Max? Or, looked at another way, why should Max be punished less severely than Paul?

It seems right that we are held to account – praised or blamed, rewarded or punished, admired or condemned – for both our actions and intentions. But should we really be held responsible for circumstances outside of our control – our good or bad moral luck? (see pp. 20–21). So in this case, should both men receive the same sentence? And if so, should the sentence be severe or more lenient?

Questions to ponder

- Attempted murder carries a lesser sentence than murder. Should that really be the case?
- Most adult males who lived in Germany during World War II fought for the Nazis. Does that make them bad people? What would you have done in their situation?
- Have you ever done something careless that might, had you been unlucky, have had terrible consequences? If the worst had happened, how might your life have changed?
- If someone is born with a naturally aggressive disposition, and into a violent and lawless family, can they really be blamed if they grow up to act in an antisocial way. After all, they chose neither their nature nor their nurture, did they?
- The French have a saying: *Tout comprendre, c'est tout pardonner* ('To understand all is to forgive all'). Do you think this is true?

₀030 WHILE THE CAT'S AWAY

Matt is a gadget nerd. Lately he has discovered surveillance cameras that connect wirelessly to his smartphone. He has rigged up several outside his house and in his backyard to discourage prowlers and burglars, but he has also placed spy cameras inside the house. These are disguised as everyday items, such as cosmetics bottles, picture frames and small ornaments. He has told his wife, Magda, and his two teenage kids, Cindy (age seventeen) and Todd (age fifteen), about the cameras outside, but not about the ones hidden inside.

For their twentieth wedding anniversary, Matt and Magda treat themselves to a weekend away without the kids. But whenever he is alone, Matt checks the secret cameras to see what the kids are up to back home. One evening he sees Cindy making out with her boyfriend in

WITH A FEW INEXPENSIVE CAMERAS LINKED UP TO A SMARTPHONE OR LAPTOP, WE CAN KEEP WATCH OVER OUR OWN HOMES. BUT ARE WE KEEPING OUR FAMILIES SAFE OR SNOOPING?

the living room, while Todd and his friends are drinking beers – his beers – and smoking joints in the den.

Matt realises he is between a rock and a hard place. If he confronts the kids with what he's seen, they will realise he has been spying on them – a breach of their privacy that will most likely ruin their relationship. And, of course, from then on, the kids will be on their guard and if they're up to no good, they'll make sure he won't find out about it.

In loco parentis

You could see the cameras as an extension of Matt's moral rights and responsibilities as a parent. He has to look out for his kids, to prevent them from going astray and possibly ruining their life chances.

Possession and use of marijuana among teenagers, while illegal in Matt's state, is not prosecuted very actively by the police, who concentrate on harder drugs and catching dealers. Nevertheless, Todd has broken the law, and Matt may therefore feel justified in confronting his son about his drug-taking.

When it comes to his daughter, however, Matt does not have the excuse of criminal behaviour. Cindy is still a minor, but she is past the age of consent in the state, and because her boyfriend is the same age, there is no question of coercion or abuse of power, which might be the case if there was a major age difference between them.

How would you resolve the situation if you were in Matt's place? For the different philosophical perspectives on the issue of surveillance, see the next dilemma.

'In [the] digital era, privacy must be a priority.'
– **Al Gore (b. 1948)**

031 BIG BROTHER IS WATCHING

Let's scale up the domestic surveillance of the previous dilemma, to consider surveillance carried out at a national level by the police and national security agencies. In addition to camera data, these organisations have access to vast amounts of personal electronic data – metadata – collected from our smartphones, tablets and computers. If Matt were head of his country's department of national security, he would have to deal with the same privacy issues he had to consider in the case of his family and the dangers inherent in revealing how he obtains information (for example, during a court hearing) so as not to tip off criminals and terrorists.

Ironically, it turns out that Matt himself has come to the attention of his country's national security agencies. He is not, in fact, a terrorist, but he shares the same name, age and rough geographical location with someone on the terrorist watch list. This is actually not such a rare occurrence in a world of seven billion people, with a finite number of birth dates and names.

SECURITY AGENCIES AROUND THE WORLD HAVE THE ABILITY TO COLLECT INFORMATION ABOUT US FROM OUR PERSONAL DEVICES. IS THIS JUSTIFIABLE IN THE INTERESTS OF KEEPING US SAFE, OR IS OUR PRIVACY MORE IMPORTANT?

Matt's smartphone and Internet data are being monitored by an automatic surveillance system. The system is programmed to alert a human operative should Matt visit certain websites, travel to certain places, meet with other 'people of interest' (others who are also under surveillance), purchase certain goods from the Internet or using his credit card, even if he should use certain words and phrases in telephone conversations, emails or social media messages.

The real Nineteen Eighty-Four

In George Orwell's dystopian novel *Nineteen Eighty-Four* (1949) video surveillance is one of the main tools employed by the totalitarian state – overseen by the mysterious figure of Big Brother – to control its citizens. According to the former CIA employee Edward Snowden (b. 1983) and computer security specialist Bruce Schneier (b. 1963), we are already living in a surveillance state, where the metadata collected from a smartphone is akin to a private detective tailing you, bugging your phone and recording all your conversations. Is this a trade-off we now have to accept in order to stay safe, or is this erosion of our right to privacy a victory for the terrorists we seek to protect ourselves against?

Better safe than sorry?

From a utilitarian perspective, surveillance cameras can be seen as making society safer, which in turn could be said to improve our happiness, making the cameras a moral good. Even curtailing the freedoms and human rights of some citizens, many would argue, is worth it if it ultimately prevents harm. What if heightened surveillance could have avoided the events of 9/11 in New York or 7/7 in London?

For Kant, however, there are rules that can never be compromised, whatever the circumstances or costs. He wrote that, 'Privacy is intrinsically good and invaluable for a free person to be autonomous and therefore to act responsibly'. In the case of Matt's domestic surveillance dilemma (see pp. 68–69), if Todd and Cindy find out they are being spied on, they will become dishonest.

℅032 SEARCHING QUESTIONS

The police are pulling over cars on a busy highway, checking them for drugs, unlicensed firearms and other illicit goods that have been smuggled into the country. They have pulled over three cars to search: The first is a BMW driven by a man in his late twenties; the second is an SUV driven by a middle-aged woman; and the third is a sedan driven by a couple in their sixties. All three drivers are black. Age and gender do not seem to be among the criteria for choosing which cars to stop; the principal or only criterion appears to be race.

Concluding that the officers are employing a form of racial profiling – targeting suspects on the basis of race – the youngest driver complains that this is a clear case of discrimination and an infringement of his human rights. The middle-aged woman is more concerned about the disruption to her working day than her human rights. She is often stopped, which she resents deeply. The older couple, in contrast, approve of such racial profiling because they have been the victims of crime committed by members of their own community, which was historically under-policed.

Thought experiment: not a black-and-white case

Risse and Zeckhauser use the following thought experiment to explore the effect of racial profiling. Imagine a country where there is no racism or social and economic disparities between different racial groups. In this society, racial profiling would not be considered offensive or hurtful and would not sour police–community relations. Now consider a country where racism does exist but racial profiling has been banned. They conclude that as the underlying racism in society is the cause of poor police–community relations, the ban on racial profiling would have little effect on levels of hurt, resentment and loss of trust in the police among those formerly targeted communities; nor would it reduce the level of racial abuse perpetrated by the police.

The true cost of racial profiling

Harvard professors Matthias Risse and Richard Zeckhauser have written a paper on the ethical case for and against racial profiling when deciding whom to stop, search or investigate. They cite the utilitarian argument that as certain crimes are committed disproportionately by members of certain racial groups, targeting these groups is not only cost-effective but necessary. However, they also argue that while it is acceptable to use race as one criterion, to use it as the only one is discriminatory and therefore immoral.

There are examples where profiling of one type or another is used without controversy. For example, age and gender profiling are routinely used in the insurance industry without causing major social problems. However, this argument does not factor in the potential damage to police–community relations when one racial group feels that it is being unfairly targeted. Unlike age and gender profiling, racial profiling compounds feelings that society is racist. Risse and Zeckhauser conclude that though qualified racial profiling is permissible, the harm caused by racial profiling is the result of underlying racism.

WITH LIMITED RESOURCES, SOME POLICE FORCES MAY ARGUE THAT TARGETING SUSPECTS BASED ON RACE IS A COST-EFFECTIVE WAY TO FIGHT CRIME. BUT IS IT LEADING TO WORSENING COMMUNITY RELATIONS?

∽033 A JUST REVOLUTION?

Imagine that your homeland is occupied by another country, ruled by an oppressive dictatorship. Although the occupiers have brought improvements in infrastructure and promoted economic development, this has been primarily in their own self-interest, and any benefits to the local population are incidental. Additionally, you are part of a majority ethnic and cultural group that is excluded from power and discriminated against in terms of access to healthcare, education and work. Any opponents of the regime are subject to arbitrary arrest, detention without trial, torture and unlawful killings.

You and your friends believe it is time to act, but you are disadvantaged by the prevailing political system and you have no access to the police or armed forces. Your only choice seems to be a terrorist campaign against the occupiers and dictatorship. You will be following many examples from history, such as the American War of Independence, the French and Russian revolutions and the apartheid struggle in South Africa, which all resorted to violence when other means failed. To their enemies, the rebels and revolutionaries were terrorists, but they thought of themselves as freedom fighters.

Ends and means

You could choose a consequentialist-utilitarian-*realpolitik* approach to justify your revolutionary actions. In its simplest form, this states that the ends (freedom from oppression) justify any means (terrorism) used to attain them. But not all philosophers agree that oppression, not even in extreme forms, justifies any form of violence against any target. Anglo-American philosopher Brad Hooker (b. 1957), for example, puts forward rule consequentialism: the view that an action is morally right only if it does not go against certain ethical rules. These are the rules that would produce the best results, if they were adopted by everyone.

The Right of Resistance

British political theorist Christopher Finlay examines the circumstances in which it is justified to invoke the Right of Resistance. He argues that if an unjust regime uses oppression to prevent people exercising their basic human rights, the oppressed have the right to resist by violent means. He defines oppression as follows:

- Domination: the subjection of one group to the arbitrary rule of another
- Harm: depriving someone of wellbeing
- Discrimination: disadvantaging one social group by another on arbitrary grounds (race, class, ethnicity or culture)
- Injustice: none of the three above are sufficient on their own without the infringement of fundamental human rights.

In the scenario above, you are subject to domination, harm and discrimination, and most importantly for Finlay, you are denied your fundamental human rights, making the regime unjust. Is your armed struggle therefore a 'just revolution'?

GROUPS FIGHTING AN ESTABLISHED STATE OR COLONIAL POWER HAVE OFTEN BEEN CALLED 'TERRORISTS'. BUT IS THE LABEL ALWAYS JUSTIFIED? WHEN DO TERRORISTS BECOME 'FREEDOM FIGHTERS'?

'The revolution is not an apple that falls when it is ripe. You have to make it fall.'
– Che Guevara (1928–1967)

034 WHAT ARE THE REALISTIC ALTERNATIVES TO NON-VIOLENCE?

Having formed the liberation movement, you are a high-ranking member of its leadership. Among those on the leadership committee who think that the ends justify the means, there are some who want to conduct a bombing campaign in the capital – the centre of power – indiscriminately targeting hotels, cafes, restaurants and malls used by civilians, tourists, local and foreign troops and government supporters and officials. Others want more focused targets: the headquarters of the secret police, government buildings and army installations.

You know from past historical examples that this has sometimes led to less than desirable outcomes, so you suggest a campaign of non-violent resistance modelled on the kind employed by Gandhi in his struggle to free India from British rule. Gandhi was a pacifist but he was not passive. The methods he advocated hurt the British economically, and in their vision of themselves as a benevolent imperial power. He employed strikes, boycotts, sit-ins and hunger strikes, but was never provoked to violence. In standing up to the bullyboy tactics employed by the British to disrupt his protests, Gandhi's stand not only demanded incredible moral conviction, but considerable physical courage.

HISTORICALLY, MOST REVOLUTIONARY STRUGGLES HAVE RESORTED TO VIOLENCE. CAN NON-VIOLENCE REALLY ACHIEVE POLITICAL AND SOCIAL ENDS AGAINST AN OPPRESSOR?

'Non-violence is the greatest force at the disposal of mankind. It is mightier than the mightiest weapon of destruction devised by the ingenuity of man.'
– **Mahatma Gandhi (1869–1948)**

The non-violent alternative

There are two shining examples of revolutionary struggles conducted by non-violent means: Mahatma Gandhi's fight for Indian independence and Martin Luther King Jr's battle for civil rights for African Americans. The two achieved their objectives and stayed true to their philosophy of non-violence, but at the greatest cost to themselves, as both men were assassinated at the moment of their triumph. They are exemplars of what French philosopher Auguste Comte (1798–1857) called (utilitarian) altruism.

Taking the moral high ground

In 1930, in full view of the world's press, Gandhi scored a major success against the British, when he led the 390-km (240-mile) Salt March from Ahmedabad to the salt-producing coastal village of Dandi. Salt was then a lucrative monopoly controlled by the British. Gandhi instructed his followers to boycott British salt and make their own. He and many of his followers were arrested and thrown into jail, but the idea caught on and millions joined the protest. When Gandhi's followers blockaded the official salt works, they were viciously assaulted by the guards, but refused to fight back, even though many were injured and killed. The world was watching, and the British lost not only money but any claim to the moral high ground.

⚘035 THREE STRIKES AND YOU'RE OUT

You are a judge, and a 'persistent offender' is about to be brought before you charged with a third felony. Your state has enacted a 'three strikes' law, meaning that, should the prosecutor demand its application, the defendant, if found guilty, will be sent to jail for twenty-five years or life. The prosecutor could choose not to invoke the law, in which case you will decide the sentence if the defendant is found guilty.

Among the key principles of the legal system, are the decrees that the punishment should fit the crime, and that the penalty should not be cruel and unusual. This particular defendant committed two serious felonies previously, but on this third occasion, his crime was the theft of property valued at around $150. Unless the three-strikes law is invoked, the defendant might face a short jail term as a repeat offender, but nothing like a twenty-five-year sentence. Can the application of the three-strikes law be said to be fair and proportionate in this case?

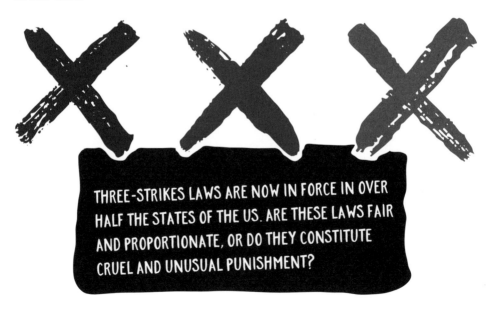

THREE-STRIKES LAWS ARE NOW IN FORCE IN OVER HALF THE STATES OF THE US. ARE THESE LAWS FAIR AND PROPORTIONATE, OR DO THEY CONSTITUTE CRUEL AND UNUSUAL PUNISHMENT?

Three-strikes hit list

According to the ACLU (American Civil Liberties Union), there are ten very good reasons to oppose the 'three strikes, you're out' principle:

1. It is an old law in new clothing: Rather than being a new approach to crime fighting, the three-strikes principle has long been used in the US and other countries.
2. It will not deter most violent crime: These types of crimes are usually not premeditated, and, because less than ten percent of serious crimes are ever solved, most violent criminals think they won't be caught.
3. It could lead to an increase in violent crime: A criminal facing a three-strikes penalty will do anything to avoid arrest; they may even kill witnesses or law enforcement officers.
4. It will clog the courts: Faced with a possible life sentence, criminals won't take plea bargains and will opt for lengthy trials, paid for from the public purse.
5. It takes away the sentencing power of judges: The courts cannot take into account any mitigating circumstances, whereas judicial discretion is a strongpoint of the US justice system. And with no parole available, the offender is not motivated to reform in prison.
6. Prison costs are becoming prohibitive: Detaining more inmates serving longer will cost more, and will not necessarily reduce overall crime rates on the streets.
7. It impacts disproportionately on minority offenders: In the US, three-strikes laws are used more often for African-American offenders.
8. It imposes a life term for non-serious crimes: The law is indiscriminate in the types of crimes that are included in the three strikes.
9. The punishment should fit the crime: The principle of proportionality is enshrined in the US Constitution: 'Excessive bail shall not be required, nor excessive fines imposed, nor cruel and unusual punishments inflicted' (Bill of Rights).
10. It is not an effective response to crime: It does not deal with the social and economic factors that can cause violent crime.

⸲036 UNDERHAND AND UNDERCOVER

Joe is a police officer working undercover. He has been given the task of infiltrating a group of political activists that are suspected of planning terrorist attacks. At present, there is no conclusive evidence that this particular group is engaging in anything other than peaceful political protest and the occasional act of vandalism, but electronic surveillance suggests that they may be planning something more violent. Using an assumed identity based on a real person, Joe has gained access to the group and become a trusted member.

In order to fit in, Joe must behave like the group members and take part in their political and social activities. These include drug-taking, casual sex with other group members, which sometimes results in pregnancy, and committing minor crimes.

The limits of policing

A recent British policing scandal revealed that undercover police officers had taken the identities of dead children in order to infiltrate groups of political activists. While they were undercover, several of the male officers had liaisons or long-term relationships with female activists, and two of the officers secretly fathered children with political campaigners under their surveillance. Having been taken off their undercover cases, the officers vanished without explanation, leaving behind their partners and children.

The first ethical issue in this case is the fact that the officers adopted the identities of real people, without the consent of their families – a form of officially sanctioned identity theft that infringes the moral rights not only of the deceased but also of their families.

The second issue is the sexual and emotional exploitation of the women, who were subsequently abandoned without explanation or financial support.

This case demonstrates that a police officer is probably not the kind of person who should be undertaking this kind of undercover work. We expect our law enforcement officers to uphold the law, not break it.

HOW FAR SHOULD POLICE OFFICERS GO IN ORDER TO 'FIT IN' WHEN THEY ARE UNDERCOVER? DO THEY HAVE THE RIGHT TO BREAK THE LAW TO PREVENT A GREATER CRIME?

Damned if he does...

As Joe chose to be a police officer, he should subscribe to the view that laws are there to be obeyed by everyone equally and under all circumstances. It is not up to a police officer to judge the validity of the law, only to apply it. Hence, Joe should not be put in the position of having to judge the morality of his actions against their consequences. However, that is exactly the position he has been put in by his employers, who are asking him to break the law in order to gather intelligence.

You could argue from a virtue-ethics standpoint that Joe is a good man who has been driven to commit evil actions in special circumstances, but doesn't his agreement to commit crime itself negate his own virtue?

WAR

'It is forbidden to kill; therefore all murderers are punished unless they kill in large numbers and to the sound of trumpets.'

– Voltaire (1694–1778)

037 IS THE IDEA OF A JUST WAR STILL RELEVANT TODAY?

As the commander-in-chief of your country's armed forces, you have the power to declare war. During the twentieth century's two world wars, your predecessors declared war on Germany and its allies. That declaration bound them to respect the conventions governing the conduct of war that both your country and Germany had signed up to. Even if these laws were not always respected, there was a legal framework to guide your and your military's actions and exact retribution in the form of legal prosecution after the war.

Today, you are just as likely to face adversaries that are not recognised as countries by other states and international organisations, and which may not have signed up to the laws of war. In fact, in their treatment of combatants and non-combatants, they may purposefully break the accepted rules of war. At the same time, they may carry out acts of terrorism on your territory and that of your allies, indiscriminately targeting the military, police and civilians.

THE MEDIEVAL JUST WAR THEORY HAS BEEN WRITTEN INTO VARIOUS CONVENTIONS THAT GOVERN THE CONDUCT OF WAR BETWEEN NATION STATES. BUT WITH THE EMERGENCE OF GLOBAL TERRORIST NETWORKS, IS THE CONCEPT STILL RELEVANT IN TODAY'S WORLD?

The rights and wrongs of just war

The two boxes on this page set out the six criteria that define a 'just war' and the four principles that should govern its conduct. First outlined in the thirteenth century by St. Thomas Aquinas, the theory of the just war has been the basis for a number of international treaties that set out laws of war, including the Hague (1899, 1907) and Geneva (1864, 1906, 1929, 1949) Conventions.

In the case that your enemy is not a country and does not recognise or respect the laws of war, does that mean that you, too, are absolved from following those laws? Most people would probably agree that to refuse to follow them would debase you to the same level as your adversary, and that you would lose all moral authority. But, as we shall see in the following dilemmas, fighting such a group highlights a host of ethical issues around just conduct in war.

Jus ad bellum – criteria of a just war

- The war must be fought for a just cause.
- The war must be declared by a lawfully recognised authority.
- The intention behind the war must be good.
- All other ways of resolving the problem must have been tried first.
- There must be a reasonable chance of winning the war.
- The means must be proportionate to the ends of the war.

Jus in bello – just conduct of war

- Noncombatants (civilians) must not be targeted.
- Only appropriate force should be used.
- This applies both to the kind of force, and how much force is used.
- Internationally agreed conventions of war must be obeyed.

₰038 KILLING COMBATANTS

You are in command of a military force sent to curb the aggressive expansionism of a country threatening one of your allies. This is not a policing action, and you have declared war after a period of failed diplomatic negotiations through the United Nations (UN). Both you and the country concerned are signatories to the international conventions on the conduct of war, dealing with the treatment of prisoners of war (POWs) and non-combatants. Your own adherence to the principles of just war means that you will not target non-combatants – though as we shall see in the dilemma on 'Collateral damage' (Dilemma 039), you may have to attack civilians in certain circumstances. As you prepare the Rules of Engagement for your armed forces, however, you ponder the ethical justifications for killing enemy soldiers.

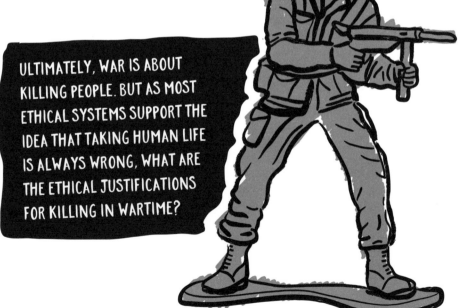

ULTIMATELY, WAR IS ABOUT KILLING PEOPLE. BUT AS MOST ETHICAL SYSTEMS SUPPORT THE IDEA THAT TAKING HUMAN LIFE IS ALWAYS WRONG, WHAT ARE THE ETHICAL JUSTIFICATIONS FOR KILLING IN WARTIME?

All things being equal

You might wish to consult the work of American political theorist Michael Walzer (b. 1935), who puts forward the argument that by choosing to be a soldier, a man has voluntarily surrendered his fundamental rights to life and liberty: first, by being a threat to other humans; second, by being a member of the armed forces, he has 'allowed himself to be made into a dangerous man'. Walzer's 'moral equality of combatants' argument has been criticised because it makes no distinction between just and unjust combatants: for example, the Allied soldiers and Waffen-SS during World War II.

A lesson from history

World War I transformed warfare, but not in the ways that the men who fought thought it would. For them it was 'the war to end all wars', but it turned out to be a foretaste of even more terrible wars to come. The Great War was the first mechanised, industrialised conflict, fought with motor vehicles, tanks, aeroplanes, machine guns, high explosives and chemical weapons. Whatever 'just cause' might have started the war in 1914, by 1916, technology had taken over – rendering the ethical guidelines developed over past centuries obsolete.

Jus in bello, the just conduct of war, states that only 'appropriate force' (meaning both the amount and type of force) can be used. But World War I saw the mass release of mustard gas that could kill and maim entire divisions. It saw the indiscriminate gassing of frontline troops and wounded soldiers who were waiting to be evacuated, as well as the medical personnel caring for them. Could this be said to be 'appropriate force'? And were the machine guns that mowed down almost 60,000 British and imperial troops on the first day of the Battle of the Somme (1 July, 1916) a proportionate use of force?

As for the fourth principle, obeying the existing conventions of war, there were no conventions that dealt with the new killing technologies and chemicals that were developed between 1914 and 1918. As with medical and scientific ethics (which we shall explore in subsequent chapters), the ethics of war have been playing catchup with advances in military technology.

☙039 KILLING NON-COMBATANTS

Your unit has been charged with intercepting and destroying a train carrying a shipment of weapons of mass destruction (WMDs), which could be used against your own military or in an attack on the civilians of your home country. The train, however, is not a military transport, but a regular scheduled service carrying hundreds of civilian passengers – men, women and children – who, according to the just war theory, should be immune from attack.

You could counter that these non-combatants have forfeited their right to life, in the same way as soldiers, because of their support for the war effort. Some of the passengers may be civilians working for defence contractors or helping the war effort in other ways.

Do you have any right to destroy the train?

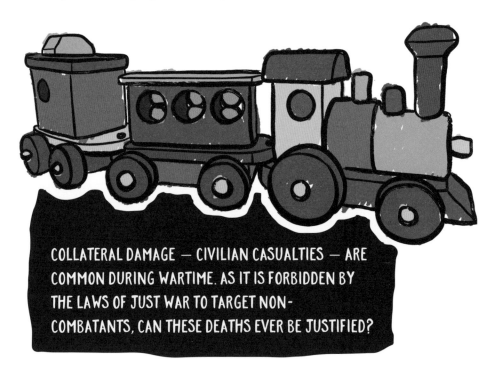

COLLATERAL DAMAGE — CIVILIAN CASUALTIES — ARE COMMON DURING WARTIME. AS IT IS FORBIDDEN BY THE LAWS OF JUST WAR TO TARGET NON-COMBATANTS, CAN THESE DEATHS EVER BE JUSTIFIED?

Double or quits

During World War II, the British philosopher Elizabeth Anscombe (1919–2001) (influenced by Aquinas) suggested a solution to the problem of collateral damage: the doctrine of double effect. This treats actions according to two types of foreseen effects: intended, and foreseen but unintended. This allows an action to have a bad outcome that was foreseen, as long as this outcome was not intended and as long as the good consequences outweigh the bad. Blowing up the train to destroy the WMDs will prevent the deaths of many innocents. Non-combatant passengers will die, but though their deaths could be foreseen, they were not intended.

Terror from the skies

If World War I had transformed the rules of just war as they applied to combatants, it was World War II that forever changed the rules that were applied to non-combatants. The first principle of *jus in bello* is that non-combatants should not be intentionally targeted. But in the age of the long-range bomber, combined with high explosives, the deliberate bombing of cities began with the German Blitz of Britain between 1940 and 1941, which resulted in the retaliatory bombing of Germany and Japan by the Allies from 1942 onwards, and ultimately the atomic bombings of Hiroshima and Nagasaki in 1945.

The bombing of enemy cities with conventional explosives could be justified by the doctrine of double effect, if the intended targets were weapons factories and other industrial sites connected to the war effort. The German and Allied bombing campaigns might have started with that aim, making any civilian casualties foreseen but unintended collateral damage. But both sides quickly realised that the terror-bombing of cities, which specifically targeted the civilian population, was a means of sapping national morale and weakening the country's ability to continue fighting.

The ultimate terror campaign was the dropping of the two atomic bombs on Japan by the Allies in August 1945. The terrifying power of the weapons was fully understood after the first successful test in July 1945. Thus, while their targets did include important military sites, the massive loss of life, which included Allied POWs, was not only foreseen but intended.

⦿ 040 REMOTE-CONTROLLED KILLING

Intelligence has located a senior member of a group that is fighting your military in the field, as well as conducting terrorist attacks against civilian targets on your home soil. He is in a house on the outskirts of a city within hostile territory, where it would be too hazardous to send in troops to arrest him. He is meeting with other group leaders at the home of one of his commanders. Also present are the commander's wife, children and members of his extended family, and civilian officials. Given the nature of the area, any attack, however well targeted, would also kill other non-combatants, who would be unlucky to be in the wrong place at the wrong time.

You have the ability to launch a precise strike against the house using drones – unmanned aerial vehicles – which would kill both the militants and the civilians. Does the main target pose a clear and present danger to you in this situation? Or would this be an extrajudicial execution? In other words, is this an act of revenge or punishment for the actions carried out by the group against your own soldiers and civilians? And would a drone strike be murder dressed up as military action?

The case against drones

Human rights groups such as Amnesty International have criticised the use of drones on the following grounds:

- Those targeted are not always combatants.
- The intelligence used to identify targets is not always reliable.
- The concept of an 'imminent threat', which is used to justify lethal action, goes far beyond legitimate self-defence.
- There is unacceptable collateral damage, without acknowledgement or any attempt at redress or compensation.
- The targeting of individuals outside a war zone is equivalent to unlawful execution.
- The alternative of capture and trial is not even considered.
- The fact that those operating the drones do so remotely creates a video-game killing culture.

In the ethical hot seat

The ethical issues raised by a drone strike were dramatised in the 2015 military thriller *Eye in the Sky*, starring Helen Mirren. The film imagines how a strike against a terrorist target might develop from a 'capture' to a 'kill' mission, and how and why those decisions would be made.

The film is a refutation of Amnesty's criticism of drone strikes. Although the damage caused by a bomb dropped from a manned military aircraft is indiscriminate, the accuracy with which a drone can be targeted could be said to make the strike more ethical, as it avoids as much collateral damage as is possible. And instead of distancing the politician and senior military that have to authorise the strike, it places them in the ethical hot seat, as they, and not a field commander, are responsible for the deployment of the drone. For example, if the strike was later deemed to be a war crime, it would be the people who had authorised it, and not the operators or launch personnel, who would be held culpable.

TECHNOLOGY IS INCREASINGLY CHANGING HOW WARS ARE FOUGHT. HOW HAS THE INTRODUCTION OF DRONES CHANGED THE ETHICAL CONDUCT OF WAR?

041 ROBOT SOLDIERS

It is a time in the near future. You are considering the development of a new generation of battlefield robots. This model would have two modes: semi-autonomous, in which the device would need human approval to engage and kill the enemy, and fully autonomous, in which the robot itself would decide who is an appropriate military target and when it is right to engage them. Your question to the developers is how does the robot decide who is and is not an appropriate target? You would not want it to turn on your own armed men, for example, or attack fleeing civilian refugees or an enemy medical facility.

In a battlefield situation, when the only people present are military personnel, then such a robot would have few ethical dilemmas to work through. But how many wars are now fought as a series of pitched battles in areas away from all civilians? I would say almost none since the end of World War II. And even in that conflict, purely military-against-military clashes were extremely rare. Wars are now fought in and around cities with large numbers of civilians, both hostile and friendly, in the firing line.

Your question to the arms manufacturer is how are you going to teach the robots right from wrong?

WHILE DRONES AT LEAST HAVE A HUMAN OPERATOR, THE MILITARY ARE NOW DEVELOPING AUTONOMOUS MILITARY ROBOTS. CAN WE EVER TRUST ROBOT SOLDIERS TO BEHAVE ETHICALLY ON THE BATTLEFIELD?

The *I, Robot* analogy

One solution, first imagined by science-fiction writer Isaac Asimov (1920–1992; see also pp. 164–165), would be to equip the battlefield robots with several basic ethical principles that they cannot break without shutting themselves down. But given the complex nature of modern-day warfare, would such an automatic shutdown turn a robot that was prohibited from harming non-combatants and behaving ethically into nothing more than a highly sophisticated and very expensive piece of mobile scrap metal? There would be constant conflict between the principles.

According to American Professor of the Philosophy of Science Colin Allen, in order for a robot to act truly autonomously, in the sense that a human being is a free moral agent, it would have to be taught a code of ethics in exactly the same way as a human being is. We learn our values from our social interactions with other humans over many years. The question, therefore, is are we so good at teaching human beings right from wrong that we could trust ourselves to instill ethical conduct in killer robots?

The *Matrix–Terminator* analogy

The second, much more dangerous possibility is that we would unwittingly create an autonomous entity that we could not control. Researcher and transhumanist Anders Sandberg (b. 1972) warns giving a robot the ability to construct its own ethical frameworks would be extremely dangerous: 'A truly self-learning system could learn different values and theories of what appropriate actions to do, and if it could reflect on itself it might become a real moral agent in the philosophical sense. The problem is that it might learn seemingly crazy or alien values, even if it starts from common-held human views.'

042 A MAD, MAD WORLD

Sally (of the latte dilemma – see pp. 12–13) is now in charge of her country's defence policy – specifically, its ageing arsenal of tactical nuclear weapons, which needs upgrading. The cost will be astronomical, but as her senior military adviser, General Bill McMann, cheerfully says, 'What price safety?' Still, Sally thinks, for the cost of the proposed new missiles, submarines and bombers, we could build new schools, universities and hospitals in every town in the country and still have change left over for a massive foreign-aid budget. But she knows exactly what he would say if she did suggest scrapping the nuclear deterrent: 'It's kept the peace these past seventy years. Yes, ma'am, can't argue with that.' No matter that the world's been transformed since 1945, and that no one in their right mind would ever launch an all-out nuclear strike as they'd be killing themselves as well as their enemies. Bill's attitude is: 'If we give up ours, what's to stop them from blackmailing us with theirs?'

Sally is going to try another tack. 'The main threat today is not from another nuclear power but from global terrorist networks', she says. 'We can't deter them with nuclear weapons. They have no cities to bomb, and they wouldn't care if they did – they want to die.' She concludes, 'And the proliferation of nuclear weapons means that, one day, the terrorists will get hold of a bomb'.

'Ah, but we can't put the nuclear genie back in the bottle, ma'am', Bill says, deploying his final killer argument.

Nuclear deterrence

As there can be no serious moral case for the slaughter of billions and the potential destruction of the planet, the main philosophical argument deployed for nuclear weapons is consequentialist: They are in themselves harmful but, by acting as a deterrent, their existence prevents a greater harm. Bill might argue this by pointing to the Cuban Missile Crisis of 1962, when 'MAD' (mutually assured destruction) saved the day by preventing either the US or Soviet Union from launching a nuclear attack.

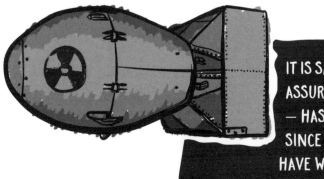

IT IS SAID THAT MUTUALLY ASSURED DESTRUCTION — MAD — HAS KEPT THE WORLD SAFE SINCE 1945. IS THIS TRUE OR HAVE WE JUST BEEN LUCKY? AND WHAT ABOUT THE ENEMIES YOU CANNOT DETER WITH ANY TYPE OF WEAPON?

'Nuclear weapons explode the theory of just war. They are the first of mankind's technological innovations that are simply not encompassable within the familiar moral world.'

– Michael Walzer (b. 1935)

043 A BUSINESS LIKE ANY OTHER

Jessica is responsible for overseeing her country's arms manufacturers: specifically, deciding who they are allowed to trade with and what they are allowed to sell. Today, Jessica is reviewing international arms export deals. But first, because she's feeling mischievous she asks her adviser, Lucas: 'Why do we need to sell arms at all? Don't you think it's immoral?'

Lucas quickly outlines the case for selling arms: 'We need a healthy, innovative arms industry to ensure our own defence in case of a military emergency; the sector provides jobs, taxes and overseas influence; our allies use their arms in self-defence and to counter crime and terrorism; and finally, if we don't do it, someone else will'.

Jessica counters, 'But can't a lot of weapons destabilise a country, if they fall into the wrong hands? They can be used for the repression of domestic opponents of a regime. And what if we sell arms to a country that we end up going to war against?'

IS THE ARMS TRADE A SPECIAL CASE, OR IS IT THE SAME AS ANY OTHER KIND OF BUSINESS, WHETHER SELLING BANANAS, CARS OR VACUUM CLEANERS?

Who can you sell to?

The trade in arms for profit is morally different from most other businesses, in that it involves not only the trade of goods, but the transfer of influence and power. Once you have sold the arms, you have the problem that they might be sold on to a third party with whom you yourself would not want to trade at all. There is no way you can monitor who the end user is or what their end purpose will be. Even if the arms are kept by the country you originally sold them to, you cannot be sure who will have access to them and how they will be used – the military could, for example, decide to mount a coup against the government using the weapons you have sold them.

The gun-seller analogy

Let's look at the arms trade in a slightly different way – after all, we're not selling white goods here but guns, tanks, planes, missiles and bombs. Imagine you have a gun shop. A customer comes in and you know for a fact that he is a convicted murderer. If you sell him a gun and he kills someone with it, aren't you an accessory to murder? You might not care if he kills someone you don't know, but what if he kills you or your wife and kids?

'Every gun that is made, every warship launched, every rocket fired signifies, in the final sense, a theft from those who hunger and are not fed, those who are cold and are not clothed.'
– Dwight D. Eisenhower (1890–1969)

044 'I WAS ONLY OBEYING ORDERS'

Imagine yourself as a young soldier fighting a guerrilla insurrection. The enemy does not wear easily identifiable uniforms and blends into the local population, only to appear suddenly to ambush you. You spend most of your time afraid, in dread of the enemy and in fear of your sergeant, who almost seems worse because he's always in your face shouting at you. You distrust your officers, the rations are bad and the weather is all wrong. You arrive in a village at dawn. No one is about. Nothing but stray animals stir.

You hear a gunshot, though you have no idea where it came from. Your officer and sergeant are shouting 'Fire! Fire!' The world goes red, blood red. An hour later, you are standing in a pile of corpses – men, women and children.

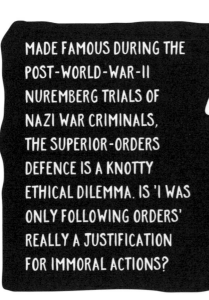

MADE FAMOUS DURING THE POST-WORLD-WAR-II NUREMBERG TRIALS OF NAZI WAR CRIMINALS, THE SUPERIOR-ORDERS DEFENCE IS A KNOTTY ETHICAL DILEMMA. IS 'I WAS ONLY FOLLOWING ORDERS' REALLY A JUSTIFICATION FOR IMMORAL ACTIONS?

Some weapons are found, but all the villagers are dead and the only casualties on your side are from friendly fire.

Even if the conflict is a just war, meaning that you are fighting on the side of the 'good guys', you have taken part in a war crime: a massacre of civilians. You could argue that in the chaos and confusion of war, you trusted your sergeant and commanding officer to make the ethical decisions – a defence that the judge might accept, given the circumstances.

The Nuremberg defence

Now imagine yourself as one of the panel of judges at the Nuremberg trials (1945–1946) after the surrender of Germany. As Hitler (1889–1945) and most of his senior command had killed themselves rather than fall into Russian or Allied hands, the defendants were lower-ranking members of the Nazi war machine and civilian government. Many of them put forward the superior-orders defence, stating that they were 'only following orders'. Considering the nature and extent of Nazi crimes, would you agree with the judges who did not accept this as a legitimate defence and sentenced the guilty to death or long prison terms?

The battlefield ethics committee

The superior-orders defence has a chequered history: accepted in some cases and rejected in others. There is no ethical system that condones the taking of human life lightly. It is always wrong to kill, though there may be mitigating circumstances that make it less unethical. But does a soldier have the capacity to examine the ethics of the orders given to him, and to decide if he can object to them on moral grounds? Drilled for obedience, he or she is less likely to question orders, especially when the price of disobedience is appearing before a court martial.

045 WAR AND PEACE

Your country is preparing to declare war. Despite several serious defeats in past conflicts, your government, influenced by a sizeable military–industrial complex that will clearly benefit from going to war, has refused to learn the lessons of its recent history.

You wish to oppose the war. What philosophical arguments could you deploy to make your case? And what actions can you take in the pursuit of your cause?

CONSIDERING THE HISTORY OF THE PAST ONE HUNDRED YEARS OF GLOBAL WARFARE, WHY AREN'T WE ALL PACIFISTS TODAY?

The deontological case: thou shalt not

The strongest case that can be made based on Kantian or faith-based deontological arguments, is that the use of violence and the taking of human life are absolute wrongs, regardless of the circumstances.

Absolute pacifists will not engage in violent resistance, which would also be contrary to their beliefs, but they can engage in non-violent protests and boycotts, and refuse to pay taxes or to contribute to the war effort.

The Quaker-inspired pacifist movements, which advocate 'turning the other cheek', are admirable, but what if your opponent carries on hitting you, no matter how many times you turn the other cheek? If his aim is to destroy you and your way of life, and your pacifism allows him achieve his aims, you are condemning survivors to lives of much greater misery and injustice than if you had resisted.

The consequentialist case: history lessons

A consequentialist might look at your country's performance in the past few major conflicts it took part in and decide that the risk of defeat is too great. We can compare this, for example, to the countries who fought in World War II. The losing Axis powers of Germany, Italy and Japan have not been involved in any major military conflicts since the end of the war in 1945. Pacifism is written into the Japanese constitution; Germany is held back by collective guilt for Nazi aggression and atrocities; and Italy's chaotic political system has prevented any further overseas adventures. Meanwhile, the victors – the United Kingdom, France, the United States and the former Soviet Union, now the Russian Federation – have been involved in one disastrous war after another. Considering the unsatisfactory outcome of most conflicts since the end of World War II, isn't it obvious that pacifism is the only sensible way forward?

Those who have a more pragmatic approach to stopping war have engaged in more aggressive and sometime violent acts of civil disobedience and sabotage, arguing that destroying a weapons factory, for example, will save lives in the long run.

The counterargument, as in the deontological case presented above, is that if a nation or group behaves in a way that goes against all civilised human values, a strong consequentialist case could be made in favour of going to war to uphold those values. Examining past conflicts, a clear example is the fight against Hitler and the Nazis, and in terms of current conflicts, the war against so-called Islamic State also has strong justifications.

'I am not only a pacifist but a militant pacifist. I am willing to fight for peace. Nothing will end war unless the people themselves refuse to go to war.'
– **Albert Einstein (1879–1955)**

046 APOLOGY CULTURE

Sally has moved from the Ministry of Defence to a new job that combines internal and external affairs. She has been asked by the head of the government to research the feasibility of a programme of apologies to be made to individuals, groups and foreign countries that her country might have injured in some way in the past. This could include individuals that have been unfairly persecuted or imprisoned; minorities who have been exploited, mistreated, dispossessed or deprived of their human rights; and foreign countries that have been attacked, invaded or colonised without just cause, or against which disproportionate force was used in war.

These apologies will be delivered by the head of state to each wronged individual, group or nation, on behalf of the state and its citizens, as well as their ancestors who committed the original crimes. It is a tricky assignment because many of the issues that the government might apologise for are still current (for example, the government might apologise for slavery, but racism is still rife). And, as the country is 240 years old this year, there is a lot of history to go through. Undeterred, Sally goes to the library and starts reading.

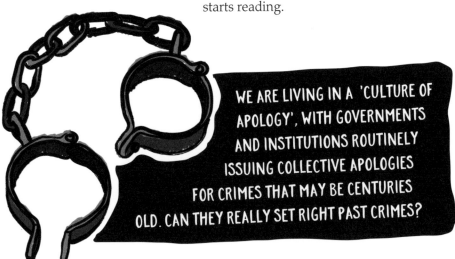

WE ARE LIVING IN A 'CULTURE OF APOLOGY', WITH GOVERNMENTS AND INSTITUTIONS ROUTINELY ISSUING COLLECTIVE APOLOGIES FOR CRIMES THAT MAY BE CENTURIES OLD. CAN THEY REALLY SET RIGHT PAST CRIMES?

An empty gesture?

According to Professor of American Studies Nicolaus Mills (b. 1938) we are living in a 'culture of apology'. But do the collective apologies delivered by governments, corporations and churches have the same value and cathartic effect as a personal apology?

Critics see them as grand sentimental gestures that are empty of any real content. In fact, rather than representing genuine atonement for past wrongs, they may mask a failure to address present wrongs. In apologising, the apologiser lays claim to the moral high ground, and forces those on the receiving end to accept the apology, even though it brings no real benefit to them. Compare personal and collective apologies in the following table:

Personal (one-to-one)	Collective (many-to-many)
• Private	• Public
• An individual takes responsibility for a specific act, expresses remorse and declares that similar behaviour will not recur.	• A group takes collective responsibility for actions against another group, and declares that similar behaviour will not recur.

Although an individual can take direct responsibility for his actions, can a group do the same thing? For example, in the case of an apology for the mistreatment of one ethnic group by another – slavery or dispossession of land, for example – the current parties are not the original perpetrators or victims, who are all long dead. Additionally, can a group that has benefited and continues to benefit from a past injustice really express remorse for something that has given them their current dominant position?

MEDICAL

'Victus quoque rationem ad aegrotantium salutem pro facultate, judicioque meo adhibebo, noxamvero et maleficium propulsabo.'
('Also I will, according to my ability and judgement, prescribe a regimen for the health of the sick; but I will utterly reject harm and mischief.')

– Excerpt from the Latin version of the Hippocratic oath

✺047 SHOULD DOCTORS BE FREE TO PRESCRIBE PLACEBOS?

You are a clinician caring for a middle-aged man who has had major surgery and is in considerable pain. The usual opiate analgesics are ineffective in controlling the man's pain, and he has asked for extra medication. A larger dose of opiates is not considered safe and may not prove any more effective, so you tell the patient that injectable saline (salt water, that is, a placebo) in combination with the painkiller has proved very effective in past cases. The saline injections produce the desired analgesic effect, relieving the patient's symptoms.

You did not lie outright but were economical with the truth. Nevertheless, the patient was reassured by your professional manner and your assertion that the placebo would work.

PLACEBOS REMAIN A MYSTERY TO MEDICAL SCIENCE, BUT IF THEY WORK, SHOULD DOCTORS BE ALLOWED TO PRESCRIBE THEM, EVEN IF IT SOMETIMES MEANS DECEIVING THEIR PATIENTS?

Placebo: the rules

- The intentions of the clinician must be benevolent, rather than for financial gain or professional advancement.
- The placebo must be given to alleviate patients' suffering, not to keep them quiet.
- When the placebo does not work, it should be discontinued.
- Placebos cannot be given if an effective treatment is available.
- The clinician should 'fess up' if asked a direct question about the nature of the treatment.
- If the placebo works and no other treatment is available, it should not be discontinued.

048 IS IT RIGHT TO USE PLACEBOS IN DRUG TRIALS?

Your teenage daughter has a terminal condition that has no cure. If she receives only palliative care, she might fall fatally ill at any time. Your doctor puts you in touch with a major pharmaceutical company that is recruiting volunteers for a clinical trial of an experimental drug that could treat your daughter's condition. The doctors explain that the purpose of the trial is to evaluate the effectiveness and safety of the new drug. They go on to explain that it will be a randomised double-blind trial, meaning half the volunteers will get the drug and the other half – the control group – will get a placebo. Even the doctors themselves will not know who receives which until the end of the trial.

You ask why they cannot give all the patients the drug, and they explain that they have to rule out the placebo effect from their results. You are desperate and this gives you some hope that your daughter might be cured, so you agree.

THE USE OF PLACEBOS IS VITAL IN TRIALS OF NEW DRUGS BUT MEANS THAT SOME PATIENTS MAY BE DENIED EFFECTIVE TREATMENT. IS IT RIGHT TO USE PLACEBOS IN DRUG TRIALS?

Means to an end

Although placebo-controlled trials are highly regulated by the Declaration of Helsinki, there remains a major ethical objection to their use, which is encapsulated in one of Immanuel Kant's most important moral precepts: that a person cannot be treated as the means to someone else's ends. In a placebo-based trial, however, those who do not receive the real drug become a means to the experimenter's ends.

☙049 TRUST ME, I'M A HEALER

Annie has a lot of minor niggling complaints: lower back pain, tension headaches, bouts of insomnia and low energy levels. She has been to see her family doctor, but after asking her a few questions about her lifestyle and daily routine, she tells Annie that she spends too much time sitting at her computer, has a poor diet, and doesn't get enough exercise, which, the doctor says, explains all her symptoms. She offers Annie some mild sedatives to help her sleep, but strongly recommends that she makes changes to her lifestyle.

Annie is not satisfied with the diagnosis. A work colleague recommends that she visits an alternative practitioner. 'I've only been going to see him for a month, and he's changed my life', she says excitedly. She rattles on about diets, treatments and manipulations that have made her feel great. 'But is he a doctor?' Annie asks. 'Oh, no', her colleague replies. 'He says doctors just dispense pills and don't understand the natural cycles of the body. He's a healer.' Should Annie follow her colleague's advice? Or should she stick to her doctor's diagnosis and recommendation?

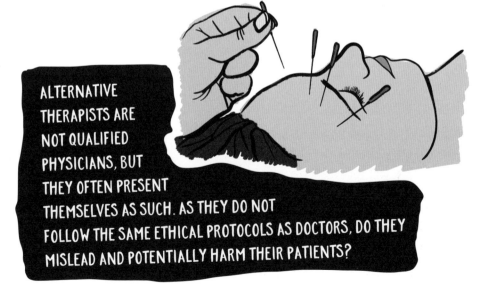

ALTERNATIVE THERAPISTS ARE NOT QUALIFIED PHYSICIANS, BUT THEY OFTEN PRESENT THEMSELVES AS SUCH. AS THEY DO NOT FOLLOW THE SAME ETHICAL PROTOCOLS AS DOCTORS, DO THEY MISLEAD AND POTENTIALLY HARM THEIR PATIENTS?

Breaking the rules

According to their medical critics, alternative practitioners are by definition unethical, even if they are well-intentioned and believe in the therapies they practice. Although many claim to be medical practitioners, strictly speaking they do not follow the four principles expected of all physicians (see below).

In terms of autonomy, they do not provide the necessary information for the patient to give his or her informed consent to a treatment. In terms of beneficence, their is little or no scientific evidence to prove these treatments offer more than emotional comfort and the placebo effect. And in terms of non-maleficence, they may prevent patients from obtaining real treatments, and subject them to ineffective or harmful ones.

Unlike a physician who is duty-bound to explain all the treatments available, and to discuss their effectiveness and side effects, the alternative practitioner usually promotes their particular therapy, whether or not it is appropriate for the patient, and whether or not there are any medically recognised treatments that would be more effective.

The ethics of doctoring

The ethical standards that all medical practitioners have to meet are laid out in the 'four principles' proposed by Tom Beauchamp (b. 1939) and James Childress (b. 1940) in *Principles of Biomedical Ethics* (1985). The four principles are:

- Autonomy: the patient's right to agree or refuse treatment through informed consent.
- Beneficence: a practitioner should always act in the best interest of the patient.
- Non-maleficence: 'First, do no harm'.
- Justice: fairness in the distribution of finite health resources, and the decision of who gets what treatment.

♻️050 SAVING AN UNBORN CHILD

Leah is pregnant. She is fourteen and had unprotected sex with her fifteen-year-old boyfriend, Carl, when they were both drunk and high. Leah's parents are 'pro-life' and want to protect the rights of the unborn child. The ideal scenario for them would be if Carl and Leah got married so that the child would not be born illegitimate. Unfortunately for them, the law in their country states the prospective parents are not old enough to get married for another two years, which means that the child will be born out of wedlock. This does not change their view that the unborn child should not be murdered.

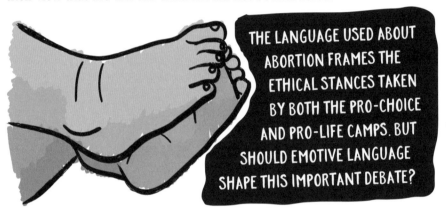

THE LANGUAGE USED ABOUT ABORTION FRAMES THE ETHICAL STANCES TAKEN BY BOTH THE PRO-CHOICE AND PRO-LIFE CAMPS. BUT SHOULD EMOTIVE LANGUAGE SHAPE THIS IMPORTANT DEBATE?

What's in a word: part I

In their choice of vocabulary, supporters of the pro- and anti-abortion cases attempt to frame their messages so that they present their arguments in the most positive light and their opponents' in the most negative. In the scenario above, Leah's parents are described as pro-life, implying that their opponents are pro-death or pro-murder. The use of the words 'unborn child' implies an autonomous existence that the word 'fetus' does not. This is reinforced by the claim that an unborn child has rights that are equivalent or superior to the mother's. Even the use of the words 'parents' and 'mother' implies relationships that may or may not exist.

Fetal personhood

The main concept deployed by those claiming that embryos have rights is the notion of fetal personhood. For many Christians, personhood is defined as having an eternal soul, which enters the body at the moment of conception. Therefore, an embryo of any age is already a person, and thus benefits from the same protections as all other human persons. British Catholic philosopher Anthony Kenny (b. 1931) believes that the moment of 'individuation', when the embryo becomes a separate being, at two weeks of age, is when it becomes a full person who should be protected.

On the other side of the debate, American philosopher Mary Anne Warren (1946–2010) sets the following criteria for personhood:

- consciousness of things and events both external and internal, and the capacity to feel pain
- the capacity to reason
- the capacity to act autonomously without external prompting
- communication, by a wide range of means, on an indefinite number of topics
- self-awareness.

This sets the bar of personhood very high and would exclude very young infants and comatose patients, who, if we followed Warren's logic, could be subjected to infanticide and euthanasia.

'It is a poverty to decide that a child must die so that you may live as you wish.'
– Mother Teresa (1910–1997)

⚯051 A WOMAN'S RIGHT TO CHOOSE

Carl's parents are horrified that their son has got his girlfriend pregnant – not because he's been having sex at the age of fifteen, which they think of as a natural part of a child's development, but because they've made a point of giving him all the facts about sex, and he should have known to use protection.

Their annoyance with their son is tempered by the fact that, as far as they're concerned, it takes two to get pregnant, and Leah is just a responsible as Carl. In fact, more so in their minds, when they discover that her parents have not taught her about contraception.

Carl's more progressive family view the situation very differently from Leah's—wanting no shotgun wedding in two years' time that they think would ruin both children's lives. They are pro-choice, and they would have no problem in obtaining a legal termination, as the girl is underage, and the fetus is less than three-months'old.

A CHANGE OF THE VOCABULARY USED TRANSFORMS HOW WE VIEW UNWANTED PREGNANCY. DOES A WOMAN HAVE THE RIGHT TO CHOOSE?

What's in a word: part II

In the second scenario, the use of 'pro-choice' implies that the opposite point of view could be termed 'pro-coercion'. Carl's parents are unlikely to talk about Carl and Leah as 'mother and father' or 'parents', because to them they are only children, incapable of taking on such roles. More importantly, the product of their union is an 'embryo' or 'fetus' and not a 'baby' or 'child'. In most developed countries, the fetus is only a potential person that does not have autonomy or personhood (see pp. 108–109); therefore it cannot have independent rights. In a non-religious ethical context, the only person who is autonomous and has rights is the woman. For Carl's parents, it's up to Leah to decide whether she keeps the baby or not.

The personal is the political

The debate on abortion rights cannot be divorced from its social and political contexts. French philosopher and feminist Simone de Beauvoir (1908–1986) and Australian feminist intellectual Germaine Greer (b. 1939) both wrote about how women were denied their sexual autonomy to serve the needs of the patriarchal order. Historically, women's reproductive rights were controlled by men, as in a patriarchal, patrilineal society, property and inheritance rights are passed through the male line. The legitimacy of children being paramount, this led to female (but not male) promiscuity being considered immoral and often criminalised.

The social emancipation of women in the twentieth century began their sexual liberation – a process that was greatly assisted by the development of reliable means of contraception under female control, such as the contraceptive pill.

'No woman can call herself free who does not control her own body.'
– **Margaret Sanger (1879–1966)**

052 IN BED WITH VANESSA

You wake up one morning, dazed and confused, in bed with virtuoso violinist Vanessa Mae – but no, it hasn't been that kind of night. An anxious group of people explain that Ms. Mae has a fatal kidney ailment, and that out of everyone in the country, you are the only person who can save her. They have kidnapped you and connected your two circulations together so that your kidneys can rid her blood of a toxin that would otherwise kill her. If you unplug yourself from her, she'll die, but if you remain connected to her, she'll recover after nine months.

THIS IS MY TAKE ON THE MOST FAMOUS THOUGHT EXPERIMENT ON ABORTION, 'THOMSON'S VIOLINIST', WITH APOLOGIES TO AMERICAN PHILOSOPHER JUDITH JARVIS THOMSON (B. 1929) AND VIRTUOSO VIOLINIST VANESSA MAE (B. 1978). WOULD YOU BE SELFLESS AND SAVE MS. MAY, OR WOULD YOU PULL THE PLUG?

Killing Vanessa

The obvious analogy to the nine months of pregnancy does not limit the experiment to female readers. On the contrary, it enables male readers to put themselves in a similar life situation. According to Thomson, you have every right to unplug Vanessa, because, although like every other human, she has a right to life, this does not mean that she has the right to use another person's body to sustain her life against that person's wishes. You are Vanessa's life-support machine, but it is up to you if you wish to sacrifice your own life for the next nine months for her benefit.

Saving Vanessa

Thomson's critics have challenged the validity of the analogy on several grounds:

- Because you were kidnapped and coerced, the only true analogy is rape.
- In most cases of conception, the woman will have consented to sex, and thus has consented to the embryo using her body.
- The woman has a duty to sustain an embryo that she voluntarily brought into being.
- Vanessa is a total stranger, but the embryo is potentially the woman's child.
- In unplugging Vanessa, you are letting her die, but in aborting a fetus, you are actively killing it.
- According to the doctrine of double effect (see p. 89), the intention of abortion is to kill, but unplugging Vanessa is merely a foreseen but unintended effect.

However, even if the woman has consented to sex and conception (or you have consented to be plugged in to Vanessa Mae), there is no reason why she or you cannot change your mind. There might be compelling reasons for this change of heart, such as a danger to your health, but that is not absolutely necessary if one accepts that the embryo (or Vanessa) has no automatic rights to the use of your body.

The valuable future argument

Another well-rehearsed anti-abortion argument, put forward by American philosopher Don Marquis (b. 1935), is that abortion deprives the embryo of a valuable future that could be like our own or much better.

This is true if the embryo develops into Vanessa Mae, but what if it grows up to be another Adolf Hitler?

053 TO TEST OR NOT TO TEST

Linda is pregnant and suffers from a genetic disorder that she has a fifty–fifty chance of passing on to her child. Her doctor strongly recommends pre-natal screening to see if the embryo has inherited the faulty gene. The condition is debilitating but does not significantly reduce the sufferer's life expectancy, though it will adversely affect their quality of life.

Linda knows that the doctor will recommend an abortion should the test be positive, and repeat abortions for future pregnancies until an unaffected embryo is produced. But Linda does not see a problem with bringing a child with her condition into the world, and she doesn't believe that our ability to screen out such children means that we ought to do it.

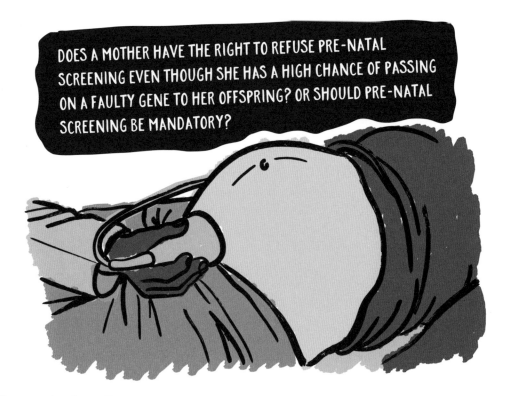

DOES A MOTHER HAVE THE RIGHT TO REFUSE PRE-NATAL SCREENING EVEN THOUGH SHE HAS A HIGH CHANCE OF PASSING ON A FAULTY GENE TO HER OFFSPRING? OR SHOULD PRE-NATAL SCREENING BE MANDATORY?

The price of knowledge

The physician and patient must take into account the following before deciding whether to go ahead with pre-natal testing:

- Prenatal screening is an important part of patient autonomy, as it gives them the information needed to decide whether to continue a pregnancy or end it.
- Information about testing and its results must be given in a non-directive and supportive manner.
- There is a small chance of a false positive, which could lead to an unnecessary abortion.
- The test is invasive and may lead to a miscarriage.

A real-world example

I am grateful for this real-life case from the BBC's *Inside the Ethics Committee*. The scenario is the same as the one on page 116, but the mother has applied for IVF (*in vitro* fertilisation) treatment, which the NHS (National Health Service) in the UK provides free of charge for three cycles.

The prospective mother has requested the treatment but refused to have any of the embryos screened for her condition. The committee have to consider three main areas: the allocation of resources, the autonomy of the mother and the future well-being of the child.

Like any other free social healthcare system, the NHS has finite resources. IVF is an expensive procedure with a relatively low success rate. If the mother's condition would further reduce the likely success rate, would they be justified in turning down her request?

The principle of patient autonomy guarantees the women's right to refuse any treatment or tests. As far as she is concerned, it is up to God to decide whether her child is born with or without the condition.

Finally, who is qualified to judge whether the child, if it does inherit her condition, will have a better or worse life than if it had been born unimpaired? The woman has a strong family support network so the child will not suffer for lack of care or resources.

Would you give her free IVF? (In the real-life case, permission was granted.)

054 HE AIN'T HEAVY...

Louis and Caroline have an infant son, Michael, who is affected by a serious blood disorder. As no treatment exists, he has a short life expectancy. There is one solution: If they had another child who was an exact tissue match, a so-called 'saviour sibling', he or she could provide a transplant that would save Michael's life.

In order to ensure a perfect match, embryos have to be fertilised *in vitro* (outside the body), screened and tissue-typed, and the embryo that is the best match is then implanted. Once the saviour sibling is born, stem cells could be transplanted from the newborn's umbilical cord, which would be discarded after birth. There is no question of using the sibling as the source of 'spare parts' for his or her brother. But some worry that saviour siblings will suffer psychological problems when or if they discover the reason for their conception.

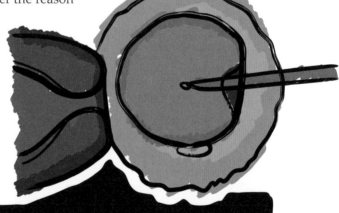

COMBINING GENETIC SCREENING AND *IN VITRO* FERTILISATION, DOCTORS CAN NOW CREATE A CHILD WHO IS AN EXACT TISSUE MATCH FOR AN AILING SIBLING. IS THIS TURNING THE CHILD INTO A COMMODITY?

The trouble with saviour siblings

There are three main areas of concern with the creation of saviour siblings: the future welfare of the child; the 'slippery slope' argument that this technology will pave the way for 'designer babies' (see next dilemma); and that, from a philosophical standpoint, it contravenes the Kantian rule that an individual cannot be used as a means to an end but only as an end in him- or herself. The saviour sibling is born as the means to save his or her sibling, and many bioethicists worry that this entails the commodification of the saviour sibling's body.

The altruistic twin analogy

Altruistic donation of organs, specifically kidneys, is a practice that rekindles one's faith in human nature. But this is not the same kind of social altruism described by Auguste Comte (see p. 77). Most commonly, altruistic organ donation is practiced by relatives and friends; so, while it is indeed admirable, it is between individuals who already have a deep emotional bond. One could compare the role of a saviour sibling with an altruistic organ donation from an identical twin or another compatible family member.

Imagine two identical twins, Melinda and Charlotte. Melinda is involved in a car crash and is rushed to hospital in a critical condition. She not only has an extremely rare blood group, but she has also suffered serious internal injuries that have compromised her kidneys. She is in desperate need of a blood transfusion and a replacement kidney. We would not be surprised if Charlotte offered both her blood and kidney to save Melinda's life.

The main difference, of course, is the issue of consent. An altruistic donation between adults presents no ethical problems, but what about the consent of a person who is not even born, and who, even once born, is too young to give their consent? The mother is presuming to give consent on behalf of an unborn child, but does she have the right to do so?

055 DESIGNING PARENTS

It is the near future. Thanks to continuing advances in genetics, the physical, mental and emotional traits controlled by an individual's genetic makeup are better understood than ever before. Kenneth and Barbara have decided to start a family and are visiting Perfect Baby Inc., where they discuss their requirements with one of the firm's genetic counsellors. For their son Ken, they request blond hair and blue eyes and a 190 cm athletic frame. They opt for enhanced athletic abilities over intelligence. For their daughter Barbie, they specify a petite brunette with green eyes and outstanding academic capabilities, preferably with an aptitude for medicine or law.

The counsellor explains how the process works: The couple's sperm and ova will be used to create their embryos *in vitro*, so that their genes can be manipulated to give the couple the children they've asked for. As long as they have their financing organised, the counsellor is happy to give them exactly what they want.

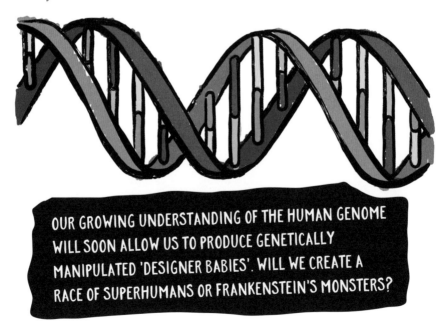

OUR GROWING UNDERSTANDING OF THE HUMAN GENOME WILL SOON ALLOW US TO PRODUCE GENETICALLY MANIPULATED 'DESIGNER BABIES'. WILL WE CREATE A RACE OF SUPERHUMANS OR FRANKENSTEIN'S MONSTERS?

'With genetic engineering, we will be able to increase the complexity of our DNA, and improve the human race.'
– **Stephen Hawking (b. 1942)**

A brave new world

In *Brave New World* (1932), novelist Aldous Huxley (1894–1963) foresaw a dystopian society in which a world state bred humanity into five castes, differentiated by physical and cognitive abilities. In the above scenario, the creation of designer babies is not overseen by the state for its own ends but by the private sector for profit. Income alone will determine who gets genetic enhancements. This could lead to the creation of a genetically superior 'class', but one that might lack genetic diversity, as parents try to achieve the optimum in appearance, intelligence and physical abilities – a world of perfect but nearly identical Kens and Barbies.

Procreative beneficence

Proposing the principle of 'procreative beneficence', Australian philosopher Julian Savulescu (b. 1963) not only encourages genetic screening, but believes that parents who currently have the opportunity to select their children should be morally obliged to do so. For example, parents who are undergoing IVF treatment can opt to have pre-implantation genetic diagnostics (PGD), but this is to screen the embryo for genetic abnormalities and defects, rather than to select for specific characteristics or to design babies, which is still beyond our capabilities. Savulescu thinks IVF-PGD should be extended to all parents so that they can select children with character traits and intelligence that will give them the best chance of achieving whatever life goals they set themselves. This would not be limited to a high IQ, but would also include such all-purpose traits as heightened empathy and improved memory.

056 HIPPOCRATIC HYPOCRISY

Case 1

A patient is having a consultation with his family doctor. He displays symptoms that are most probably benign but could also indicate a much more serious but rare condition. Knowing this patient to be the litigious type, the doctor orders a battery of invasive tests and procedures that are not only very unpleasant for the patient, but also extremely expensive. A week later, the patient is given the all-clear; his symptoms were probably indigestion or colic.

Case 2

A patient is referred to a surgeon for a complex surgical procedure, with a high risk of failure made even worse because the patient is both elderly and obese. After reviewing the case, the surgeon decides not to operate on the patient, even though her life expectancy and quality of life will be severely curtailed without the operation.

WE LIVE IN LITIGIOUS TIMES, AND THE MEDICAL PROFESSION IS NOT IMMUNE FROM LAWSUITS. MUST DOCTORS PRACTICE 'DEFENSIVE MEDICINE' TO AVOID BEING SUED?

Assurance and avoidance

In response to an increase in malpractice suits, doctors are resorting to assurance and avoidance behaviours. Assurance (case 1) is ordering unnecessary tests and services, and avoidance (case 2) is when a physician or health provider refuses to take on high-risk patients.

After being sued, one physician claimed that he had been forced to become 'a bad doctor', as he now felt he was in breach of the four principles that underpin medical ethics: autonomy, beneficence, non-maleficence and justice (see p. 109).

Real-life lawsuit

In 2005, a middle-aged man visited his doctors requesting a screen for prostate cancer. Prostate cancer is asymptomatic and there was no history of the disease in his family, but the man had seen a documentary about it and was now worried. The doctor performed a rectal examination but could find no sign of abnormality. He explained that there was a blood test to measure PSA (prostate-specific antigen), which could indicate the presence of the disease, but that the test returned many false positives, as elevated PSA levels were also associated with other benign prostate disorders. The patient opted to have the blood test.

When the doctor received the results, they were inconclusive. His PSA levels were slightly elevated but not within the range that would indicate a high likelihood of cancer. The next stage would involve a prostate biopsy, a procedure not to be undertaken lightly, as it can have very serious side effects, including rectal pain, bloody urine and semen, erectile dysfunction and infections of the skin or urine that would require hospitalisation. After a lengthy discussion, the patient took his doctor's advice and did not have the biopsy.

Unfortunately, in 2007, the patient was screened again at another clinic, and this time his PSA levels were such that a biopsy was considered necessary. Prostate cancer was confirmed and treated and the patient went into remission. He sued the first doctor and the clinic for malpractice.

Would you award damages against the clinician in this case? (The court's decision was that the doctor was not personally liable, but that his clinic was.)

⟡057 LIVE AND LET DIE

Anna-Lise (see pp. 18–19) did not commit suicide while she was still healthy, and now she has succumbed to a serious illness, which robs her of any remaining quality of life. She is in the hospital and in considerable pain, which she cannot always control with medication. The law in her state has not changed, but she is now too unwell to travel to a state or country where assisted suicide is legal.

Her only choice is passive voluntary euthanasia (right to die) by refusing lifesaving treatment in person or by writing an advance health directive, indicating her wishes should she need lifesaving treatment in the future but be unable to withhold her consent because she is in a coma or has lost mental capacity. Unfortunately, this situation has not occurred. This leaves her with two unpleasant alternatives: attempt suicide in her weakened state or starve herself to death.

EUTHANASIA IS THE MOST CONTESTED ETHICAL ISSUE IN MEDICINE TODAY. IS LETTING SOMEONE DIE REALLY SO DIFFERENT FROM ASSISTING THEM TO DIE?

Arguments against legalising active euthanasia
- The elderly and terminally ill may be psychologically vulnerable.
- The high costs of healthcare may motivate patients.
- Using 'substituted judgement' (where doctors or family members make decisions on behalf of the patient) may not work where there is conflict between the patient and the decision-maker. There may be prejudice against citizens with disabilities.
- Expanded definitions of 'terminal illness' may include a range of people not now included.

Types of euthanasia
- Voluntary euthanasia (right to die) – legal in many jurisdictions
- Non-voluntary euthanasia (without patient's consent) – legal in some jurisdictions, when the next of kin can make the decision on behalf of an incapacitated patient who has not made a living will.
- Involuntary euthanasia (against patient's will) – illegal, usually considered to be murder

These three types of euthanasia can be further subdivided into:
- passive euthanasia (withholding lifesaving treatment)
- active euthanasia (use of lethal substance or force)

Thought experiment: Smith and Jones

If their six-year-old cousin dies, Smith and Jones will get a large inheritance. The pair decide separately to murder the boy to inherit the money. In one scenario, Smith waits for his young cousin to have a bath, sneaks into the bathroom, drowns him and makes the death look accidental.

In the second scenario, Jones also waits for his cousin to have a bath, but as he enters the bathroom to drown him, he finds the cousin has slipped, knocked himself out and is lying face down in the water. Instead of helping him (or making sure that he will drown by holding him under), Jones lets the cousin drown, thereby accomplishing the deed without active intervention.

With this thought experiment American philosopher James Rachels (1941–2003) attempts to demonstrate that there is no moral difference between Smith's active killing of his cousin by drowning, and Jones's passive inaction in letting his cousin drown – each of them are equally morally responsible for the boy's death. He concludes that active euthanasia (killing) is no different from passive euthanasia (letting die).

⸮058 LIFE FOR LIFE'S SAKE

Mary is in the room next door to Anna-Lise's. She suffers from several serious conditions, any one of which could kill her. She, however, is not alone in the world, and has three loving daughters, all married with children, who visit her daily. When Mary has too many visitors at once, one or two of them wait in Anna-Lise's room. Today it is Mary's eldest daughter, Kate, who is waiting for her turn. She tells Anna-Lise that Mary's condition is getting worse. She has to be fed through a tube into her nose, and a ventilator now assists her breathing. She is so full of drugs to control her pain that she is barely conscious. 'The doctors want to

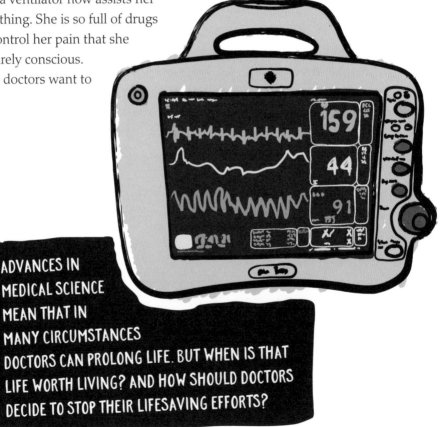

ADVANCES IN MEDICAL SCIENCE MEAN THAT IN MANY CIRCUMSTANCES DOCTORS CAN PROLONG LIFE. BUT WHEN IS THAT LIFE WORTH LIVING? AND HOW SHOULD DOCTORS DECIDE TO STOP THEIR LIFESAVING EFFORTS?

stop feeding her and turn off the ventilator', Kate says. 'What do you think we should do?' Anna-Lise doesn't know what to say. She wishes she were as ill as Mary, or that she had a legion of relatives to come and visit her. With no advance health directive, the family must decide for Mary.

'But that's horrible, don't you think?' Kate asks. 'If she doesn't die when they turn the ventilator off, they'll let her die of dehydration and starvation. I wouldn't treat a dog like that, so why do we think it's OK for humans?'

Anna-Lise thinks back to when her own mother had died of cancer over fifty years before. Things were different then. There were few treatments, and the disease had run its course quickly. But there had been a lot of pain. One evening the doctor had taken her to one side and said, 'Shall I give her something to ease the pain and help her on her way?' And Anna-Lise had understood immediately what the doctor meant. She held her mother's hand as the doctor injected a clear liquid into her arm. A few minutes later her mother's breathing eased, her face relaxed for the first time in weeks, and she slipped away peacefully.

Quick and painless

Though he was opposed to any form of euthanasia, American philosopher James Rachels argued that there was no rational basis for the distinction between active and passive euthanasia – killing and letting die – which he found to be morally equivalent.

Doctors justify passive euthanasia by using the doctrine of double effect: If treatment, ventilation or feeding are withdrawn, death is a foreseeable consequence but it is not the intention (which, of course, it is).

In a case like Mary's, Rachel suggested that active euthanasia would be preferable to passive euthanasia because, if the doctors wished to end her suffering in the most humane way, an injection of a lethal dose of a painkiller would be much faster and cause less suffering than letting Mary starve to death or suffocate.

૭059 ORGANS FOR SALE

Max's kidneys have failed. He survives on daily dialysis, but to live a full life again he needs a kidney transplant. With over 100,000 people on the waiting list, his chances of getting a kidney through conventional channels are slim. He had hoped for an altruistic donation from a close friend or family member, but no one is a good enough match. He has even considered buying a kidney on the black market, but decided against it when he heard about the unethical ways organs are obtained.

Would a regulated market in organs be the answer for Max and many millions waiting for transplants worldwide?

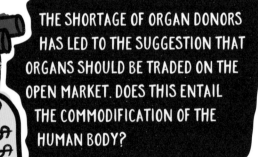

THE SHORTAGE OF ORGAN DONORS HAS LED TO THE SUGGESTION THAT ORGANS SHOULD BE TRADED ON THE OPEN MARKET. DOES THIS ENTAIL THE COMMODIFICATION OF THE HUMAN BODY?

'The most publicly justifiable application of human cloning, if there is one at all, is to provide self-compatible cells or tissues for medical use, especially transplantation.'
– Julian Savulescu (b. 1963)

Analogy: to toss or not to toss

Critics of organ sales claim that it would displace or reduce altruistic donations, and raise issues of consent, exploitation, instrumentalisation and objectification of the seller. But an analogy suggested by British law professor Susan Millns (b. 1967) might give Max some hope. Very similar issues were raised in the case of a dwarf who tried to overturn a French ban on 'dwarf tossing', which was prohibited on the grounds that it diminished the human dignity of both the tossers and the tossed.

The 'dwarf' concerned argued that he gave full consent to being 'tossed', and was not exploited, objectified or instrumentalised by the activity, which took place in nightclubs for the entertainment of clubbers. In fact, he said, to outlaw dwarf tossing was tantamount to depriving him of his livelihood, and was therefore an assault on his human dignity rather than its protection. To put his argument in philosophical terms, because he was tossed by friends and for his own profit and enjoyment he was not a Kantian means to an end, but an end in himself who had not sacrificed his human dignity.

Send in the clones

Bioethicist Julian Savulescu has proposed a far more radical solution to alleviate the shortage of organs for transplantation: human cloning. The cloning of human embryos for research purposes is currently illegal in most countries, but as Savulescu points out, 'One in 300 pregnancies involves clones', that is, the natural production of identical twins, which are, in fact, clones. The cloning of farm animals is now routine, as is the cloning of human stem cells for therapeutic use. There would be no difficulty in cloning a human being by splitting an early embryo into identical twins. One of the clone-twins could be frozen but later allowed to develop to be used as a source of cells, tissues and organs for transplantation into the adult 'original'.

As we already allow the abortion of embryos for social reasons, wouldn't their use for lifesaving treatments and transplantation be not only morally permissible but actually a moral necessity?

SEXUAL

'When I'm good, I'm very good,
but when I'm bad, I'm better.'
– Mae West (1893–1980)

060 A MATTER OF CONSENT

Vince and Carla are having sex on a regular basis. There has been no coercion or violence on either side, or from a third party, and no money or other material inducement has been offered or received by either party. Their sexual relationship is discovered by their parents. What happens next?

The one criteria that usually determines the legality and morality of a sexual relationship is the age of the participants, that is, whether both participants are capable of giving their full informed consent to have sex. Let's examine three possible cases:

Case 1: underage sex
Both Vince and Carla are fourteen and therefore underage in their country. As they are the same age, however, there is no question of a legal prosecution in these circumstances.

Case 2: one partner is underage
This could be much more serious for the older party, if there is a large difference of age. But the pair are within two years of one another: Vince is fourteen and Carla is sixteen. The matter is made more complicated, however, because Carla is a summer camp counsellor and Vince is one of her campers. Although Carla is in a position of trust, this is mitigated by their closeness in age.

Case 3: two partners are over the age of consent
No problem, you may think. But what if Vince has an intellectual disability and Carla does not. How does that change the consent arithmetic?

The ethics of sex

Philosophers are perhaps not the best people to consult on sex. The ancient Greeks had no age of consent (for boys), and relationships between adult men and adolescents were the norm in the age of Socrates (c. 469–399 BCE) and Plato (c. 423–347 BCE), while for Kant, sex was only morally right within a marriage between a man and a woman. For French philosopher Michel Foucault (1926–1984), the age of consent was a cultural fiction that merely served to control certain groups in society.

As far as sex is concerned, a great deal has changed in the past twenty years. Ages of consent have changed in many countries, equalising the ages for men and women, and for heterosexuals and homosexuals. Setting religious beliefs and cultural norms aside, the issue that must be decided is whether both parties have the capacity to give their consent to the sexual acts they are participating in. In Case 1, either both Vince and Carla have capacity or neither do; therefore, there is no morally culpable person. Case 2 is more complex because Carla is in a position of trust, but the two are close in age. Case 3 throws up real problems: although he is of age, does Vince have the mental capacity to consent to sex with Carla?

THE AGE OF CONSENT IS ONE OF THE MOST HOTLY DEBATED AREAS OF SEXUAL ETHICS. WHAT IT REALLY BOILS DOWN TO IS: WHO CAN CONSENT TO HAVE SEX?

061   THE LIMITS OF CONSENT

Vince and Carla are now adults, and they are now married. They have become more adventurous with their sexual experimentation, and they are trying out BDSM (bondage, discipline, sadism and masochism), a set of sexual practices that include power exchange; role-play, including simulated rape, kidnap, imprisonment and race play; simulated and real punishments, some of which can result in injuries; the use of verbal abuse and humiliation; and the use of clothing and equipment that might be considered offensive (or even illegal), including Nazi symbols, uniforms and regalia.

In one particularly adventurous session, Carla, who is the dominant partner, inflicts a savage flogging upon Vince, causing considerable bruising to his back and buttocks. At his request, she also brands one off his buttocks with a spoon she has heated up on the stove.

Unfortunately for the couple, Vince's 'brand' becomes badly infected and requires him to attend the local A&E. Carla drives him to the hospital and waits with him as he is treated. Seeing the nature of his injuries, the A&E staff call the police, who immediately arrest Carla for battery.

The couple's defence is that there was no assault, as the injuries Vince sustained were part of a consensual BDSM encounter, within the bounds of a loving relationship between spouses.

THE RECENT SUCCESS OF *FIFTY SHADES OF GREY* HAS MADE PUBLIC THE WORLD OF BDSM AND ENCOURAGED MANY TO TRY OUT 'KINKY SEX'. IS THERE A LIMIT TO WHAT YOU CAN CONSENT TO?

Abuses of power

The few cases that have gone to trial have provided inconsistent precedents. A trial of a group of gay men in the UK found the defendants (both the men performing the acts and those receiving them) guilty of assault, rejecting the argument of consent in favour of a more conservative stance that questioned the morality of homosexuality as much as BDSM.

A subsequent case a decade later, which involved the branding of one spouse by another with a heated spoon, was thrown out by the judge on the grounds that the matter was private and the participants were a married couple.

Philosophically, we are back in dwarf-tossing territory, with one side arguing that such actions are demeaning to human dignity and cannot be consented to – the Kantian argument of means and ends. Vince was a means to Carla's end – her own sexual gratification. However, Vince could argue that he obtained as much satisfaction from the branding as Carla; hence, he was not a means but an end in himself.

Thought experiment: the boxing match

Let's take Vince and Carla out of the bedroom and place them in the boxing ring. Carla is the better fighter, and during the match Vince receives considerable bruises to his face and body. When she knocks him out, he falls and injures himself. Why is it OK for Carla to injure Vince in a boxing match and not in a consensual BDSM interaction?

'S & M is the eroticisation of power.'

– Michel Foucault

⟅062 A POINT OF PRIDE

Bill and Dick were married last year, and this autumn they are expecting their first child thanks to a surrogacy arrangement with a lesbian friend. The couple enjoy the same pensions, health benefits and inheritance rights as a married heterosexual couple. Although it's true that homophobia still exists in the world and in the country in which they live, in their state, in terms of their rights and protections afforded to them by the law, Bill and Dick are now equal with heterosexuals in every respect. What is the point of 'gay pride' now? Should we be moving on to celebrate 'human pride'?

THE TRANSFORMATION OF LGBTQ RIGHTS OVER THE PAST DECADE HAS BEEN SO FAR-REACHING THAT THE WHOLE CONCEPT OF 'GAY PRIDE' CAN SEEM OUTMODED. HAS THE TIME COME TO PUT AWAY THE RAINBOW FLAGS?

Unnatural law

The historical case against gay sex is based on ancient doctrines of natural law dating back to antiquity, to Plato and redefined by St. Thomas Aquinas in the Middle Ages. Natural law claims that the only moral function of sexual intercourse is sex for procreation. This automatically places LGBTQ sex beyond the bounds of morality, and by extension, makes any gay relationship and many unmarried straight relationships immoral. It also damns straight married couples who are childless and who have passed the age of procreation – sorry, folks, you can't have fun anymore. Get thee to a nunnery or a monastery!

Born this way

When the Gay Liberation movement emerged in the 1970s, the basis for the call for equal rights and protection from discrimination was that homosexuality, bisexuality, lesbianism and transgenderism did not consist merely of a set of sexual practices that men and women chose to engage in, but were innate sexual identities that they had no control over: they were born gay, lesbian, bisexual or trans; they did not wake up one morning and decide to spice up their sex lives. If homosexuality is a genetic trait, in the same way as height, sex, and eye, hair and skin colour, homophobia is exactly the same as racism and sexism. But though there are repeated reports in the media that the 'gay gene' has been identified, these claims are either false or grossly oversimplify the research findings presented. Geneticists concede that even if it is an inherited trait, sexuality will not be controlled by one gene, but by many in interaction with the environment.

A constructive approach

Michel Foucault sees sexualities and sexual identities as fluid, evolving and 'socially constructed'. In classical Athens, for example, age-graded relationships between men and boys were the social norm. During the medieval period homosexuality was banned as a sin and a crime. Today LGBTQ people have won legal equality, but not universal acceptance. Whether homosexuality is the product of nature or nurture is largely irrelevant. What matters is how it is understood in any given period and culture; this defines whether it is accepted, merely tolerated or condemned.

'Homosexuality began to speak on its own behalf ... using the same categories by which it was medically disqualified.'
– Michel Foucault

⚲063 GENDER TROUBLE

Sally is six when she announces that she is not a little girl who wants to play with dolls but a little boy who wants to play with toy lorries, and that she wants to be called Nathan. 'She's always been a bit of a tomboy', Sally's mother says to her husband. 'She won't ever wear anything pink or frilly.'

Sally's father doesn't know what to say – 'But she's a girl!' won't cut it, so he keeps quiet. 'I've been reading about it online', his wife goes on. 'She's "trans" – –a boy born in a girl's body.'

It's not natural, he thinks to himself, as his wife prattles on about surgery and hormone pills. Mind you, he has always wanted a son, so why not?

OUR UNDERSTANDING OF GENDER IS CHANGING, CREATING WHOLE NEW GENDER IDENTITIES: TRANS PEOPLE, WHO DO NOT NECESSARILY FIT WITHIN OUR BINARY MALE/ FEMALE CATEGORIES. IS IT TIME TO RETHINK GENDER ALTOGETHER?

The performance of your life

Many trans people believe that they have been born with the wrong gender – or in the wrong body – which they believe can be corrected by reassignment surgery. This conflicts with contemporary sociological views of sexuality and gender. Michel Foucault (see previous dilemma) argued that sexuality was socially constructed by the interplay of cultural norms and individual experience.

In *Gender Trouble* (1990), Judith Butler argued that gender is 'performative', that is, that it is not somehow inscribed in the body, but has to be created by repeated 'performances' of masculinity or femininity. She cited the examples of female impersonators who 'perform' femininity but are not female and, for the most part, do not want to become women. Like other social constructionists, Butler sees the body as gender-neutral until it is shaped by the self in response to pre-existing social models.

The right not to choose

Although many trans people are fighting to be allowed to live as the opposite, there are also people who might be identified as trans who are in fact 'intersex' (with sexual characteristics associated with both sexes), and who would prefer not to belong to one of the accepted binary categories of male or female.

The case of South African athlete Caster Semenya (b. 1991) illustrates the difficulties faced by an individual with a contested gender. Questions were raised about her biological sex after her victory in the Women's 800 Metres in several major competitions in 2009. She was tested that year, and though the results were never made public, leaks suggested that she was intersex. As a professional athlete of some note, and in order to continue her competitive career, she must be either male or female. Semenya has not expressed a desire to change her gender or to claim some kind of intermediary status. She may have intersex characteristics, but her gender identity is undeniably female.

Does the performativity of gender allow her to choose to remain female? Or does the issue of fairness to her fellow competitors mean that she should be declared male, or excluded from the competition altogether?

⸉064 THE OLDEST PROFESSION

Case 1: the high-class escort

Charlotte began her career as a sex worker to finance her studies at a prestigious university. After graduating, she decided to continue rather than find a full-time job. She works independently through websites with a high-class clientele. For extra security, she works out of an expensive downtown apartment with two other escorts.

Case 2: feeding a habit

Unmarried mother Carly became addicted to drugs when she was a teenager. She ran away from home aged sixteen and hooked up with an older man who turned out to be a pimp. Although she has tried to get on the straight and narrow, she is caught in a cycle of deprivation, drug abuse and exploitation.

Case 3: trafficked for sex

Carlotta was lured into the country with the promise of a full-time job, only to find that her so-called employer was a brothel. She feels trapped, as the brothel keeper tells her that if she goes to the cops, she'll be thrown into jail as an illegal migrant.

ATTITUDES TO FEMALE SEX WORKERS HAVE CHANGED DRAMATICALLY SINCE THE SEXUAL REVOLUTION OF THE 1960S. WHAT'S SO BAD ABOUT SELLING SEX?

Feminists against

You might imagine that the strong belief in women's autonomy and self-ownership that makes many feminists such prominent supporters of abortion rights would also make them sympathetic to female sex workers. But prostitution is one of the most contentious issues splitting the contemporary feminist movement. Radical feminist Andrea Dworkin (1946–2005), for example, wrote that, 'Prostitution in and of itself is an abuse of a woman's body'. She went on to say, 'In prostitution, no woman stays whole'.

The abuse, violence and exploitation that many female sex workers (like Carly and Carlotta) face mean that there can be no meaningful consent. The practice of prostitution is seen as demeaning to human dignity, as well as physically and mentally harmful. The prostitute is exploited, instrumentalised and objectified to become the means to her clients' ends.

Feminists for

Feminist supporters of prostitution counter that prostitution can be empowering to women and give them economic independence from men. They could point to the case of Charlotte who is a sex worker by choice. She is not trapped in a violent abusive lifestyle, and though she may be objectified and instrumentalised by her clients, at the rates she charges, she might be exploiting them!

The problem is that for every Charlotte working safely by choice, there are probably hundreds of Carlys and Carlottas who are trapped in a lifestyle they didn't choose. Should we curtail Charlotte's freedom to protect those less fortunate?

'To the moralist prostitution does not consist so much in the fact that the woman sells her body, but rather that she sells it out of wedlock.'
– **Emma Goldman (1869–1940)**

✺065 BOYS WILL BE BOYS

Case 1: the male escort

Chad is a successful male sex worker employed by women and gay and bisexual men. At 190 cm and 90 kg, and with a background in the military, he has never felt threatened, exploited or abused, and he's not sure what 'instrumentalised' means. His clients are understandably very respectful. Hampered by a lack of academic qualifications and with few career options, he chose escorting over low-paid manual or retail work.

It could be argued that Chad has become the means of his clients' ends, but Chad could counter that not only does he benefit financially from his work, he enjoys it.

Boys will be boys

Male sex workers have always existed in one form or another. And they have always been treated differently from their female counterparts. If they have been reviled in the past, it is probably more to do with prevalent attitudes to homosexuality than to their chosen profession, while female sex workers are damned twice: by their gender and their profession.

Historically, and still in some jurisdictions today, the male client of a female sex worker is let off, while it is the woman who is arrested and criminalised. Fortunately, this is now changing. If we are to attach any legal or moral censure to prostitution, who should receive the larger share: the client or the sex worker?

Case 2: the film star

A Hollywood A-lister is caught with his trousers down in a car with a female sex worker he has just picked up on the street. For once, his fame has not saved him from embarrassment and he is exposed in the media.

Both the actor and the sex worker are arrested and charged, but while the sex worker earns considerable sums from selling her story to the media, the actor has his reputation dragged through the mud, and probably loses income because he will be passed over for certain roles while the story is on the front pages.

DEBATES ABOUT PROSTITUTION OFTEN SEEM TO BE ALL-WOMEN AFFAIRS, AS IF THERE ARE NO MEN INVOLVED. WHAT ABOUT THE MEN IN THE STORY – THE CLIENTS AND MALE SEX WORKERS?

The female eunuch

Germaine Greer's famous book *The Female Eunuch* (1970) was one of the seminal texts of second-wave feminism. In it, Greer argues that while a woman cannot become a eunuch because she doesn't have a penis to remove, women have long been denied their sexual freedom and autonomy, to the point where taking pleasure from sex is deemed immoral.

Is the female sex worker also made into a eunuch? On the one hand, she has the freedom to engage in sex with multiple partners, but on the other, she is obliged to engage in sex with multiple partners to make a living. Ultimately, it depends on whether she needs to take every job and submit to whatever the client wants, or whether she has the choice to refuse clients and their requests, and whether, like male sex worker Chad, she enjoys her work.

066 PORN REINVENTED

Scene 1: role reversal

A man and a woman are filming a scene for a porn website. The two actors are there of their own free choice and are well remunerated for their day's work. But this is not what you'd call 'traditional' porn, where the female actor is the object of desire. In this scene, it is the woman who is dressed and the man, naked. She is a dominatrix using the man's body for her own pleasure in an erotic reversal of the usual gender roles. The film crew and director, who also run the website, are women, and their target market are members of the BDSM community of both sexes.

Scene 2: girl-on-girl action

Two women are filming a scene for another porn website. As in Scene 1, there are no issues of consent, coercion or exploitation. The subject might appear to be more conventional—girl-on-girl action is a staple theme of porn produced for heterosexual men – but this website is aimed not at straight men, but at lesbians and bisexual women.

PORNOGRAPHY HAS MOVED ON SINCE IT WAS THE TARGET OF FEMINIST FURY IN THE 1980S. IS TWENTY-FIRST-CENTURY PORN STILL SEXIST?

No sex please, we're feminists

Although many feminists see pornography as part of the patriarchal system that oppresses women, others see it as potentially empowering women, by offering alternative models of sexuality. Thanks to the Internet, the variety of pornography now available has challenged dominant straight views of gender and sexuality, and pornography itself needs to be redefined. As pro-sex feminist Ellen Willis (1941–2006) observed, obscenity is in the mind of the beholder: 'What turns me on is erotic; what turns you on is pornographic'.

Moral panic

For many, the problems with pornography stem not from who makes it and who it's made for, but from its mode of delivery. In the magazine/cinema age, porn of any kind was difficult to access, especially for minors. It became easier in the video age, but you still had to be old enough to buy videos and able to pay for them. Today, anyone with a PC, tablet or smartphone, regardless of age or earnings, can access almost any type of porn with a few search words, or even by accident.

One consequence of Internet porn's high visibility is that it has become the subject of a 'moral panic', the porn being blamed as the cause of sexual violence against women and the sexual abuse of children. But these problems existed before the Internet. Has the Internet made them worse, or are we scapegoating porn as an easy explanation for a complex social issue?

'Pornography, in the feminist view, is a form of forced sex, a practice of sexual politics, and institution of gender inequality.'
– **Catherine MacKinnon (b. 1946)**

⧡067 THE MORE THE MERRIER

Arthur and Beth are in bed enjoying a Sunday morning lie-in. They've been together for three years and have been discussing having a child. Mark walks in carrying a tray of coffee and pastries, which he sets down on the bed before climbing in beside Arthur and Beth. The three have long ago given up trying to explain their polyamorous relationship to their more conventional friends, who don't seem to be able to take the arrangement for what it is: the consensual sexual and emotional union of three adults. Some of their friends ask if the two boys are 'gay', or if one of them is and is just playing along so he can share the girl with his buddy. It used to annoy them but now they just smile and change the subject.

Of course, if they do have a child, it will complicate the situation. The law currently favours couples in terms of parenting rights, as a child can only have one legal 'father' and one legal 'mother'.

HISTORICALLY, THE MONOGAMOUS UNION OF A HETEROSEXUAL MAN AND WOMAN HAS BEEN THE BASIS FOR THE ETHICS OF RELATIONSHIPS IN THE WEST. BUT HAS HETEROSEXUAL MONOGAMY HAD ITS DAY?

Historical precedents

In cultural and historical terms, patrilineal (inheritance through the father) heterosexual monogamy has not been the dominant mode of organising reproductive and inheritance rights within society. Many scholars believe that during prehistory, matrilineal (inheritance through the mother) systems predominated, and were slowly replaced by patrilineal systems as societies and gender roles evolved. Additionally, heterosexual monogamy has had to contend with heterosexual polygamy (one husband with several wives) and heterosexual polyandry (one wife with several husbands). Although never dominant in any culture, homosexual relationships have also played an important role in the education and socialisation of boys, and have been recognised as alternative or complementary to heterosexual relationships.

The law lags behind

The contemporary alternatives to heterosexual or homosexual monogamy are bisexuality and polyamory (a relationship between three or more consenting adults). In *Marriage and Morals* (1929), British philosopher Bertrand Russell (1872–1970) wrote that notions of sexual morality were no longer valid after the advent of effective methods of contraception. Although Russell was only advocating pre-marital heterosexual sex to see if partners were compatible, the book created a storm of protest and led to his dismissal from a teaching post in the US. All he was pointing out, however, was that the law had not kept up with the social and technological changes that were transforming sexuality.

'Bisexuality immediately doubles your chances for a date on Saturday night.'
– **Woody Allen (b. 1935)**

⸻068 CYBER CHEATS

Forty-five-year-old Seth is having a wild affair with Annie that has been going on for about a year. His wife, Martha, discovers the affair by accident when the latest computer system upgrade accidentally syncs Seth's tablet with her laptop. She is shocked to discover their explicit online chats and exchange of intimate photographs. According to her online profile on 'SugarBabes.com', Annie is a twenty-year-old university student, who is looking for a 'Daddy type who knows how to spoil his little girl (kiss, smiley face, pouting face, kiss, kiss)'.

Martha discovers that not only has Seth been engaging in wild cybersex sessions with Annie, but he's been sending her gifts: nothing major so far, but, she notices, what started as trifles costing a few pounds, such as flowers and chocolates, are now more substantial presents costing £40 to £50 – and Annie has been talking about needing to replace her car!

An outraged Martha confronts her husband that evening when he gets back from work. She tells him to break it off with Annie that very evening, or she's going to file for divorce. A distraught Seth goes online but discovers that Annie's profile has been taken down by the website. It turns out that 'Annie' was in fact a Russian Internet fraudster called Ivan, who conned gullible middle-aged men to send him money once he had won them over with steamy cybersex chats and fake pictures.

Thou shalt not...

When Martha finds out about Ivan, she doesn't stop laughing for three days. And she's pretty sure that Seth's online romancing days are over. From a consequentialist viewpoint, the only person he's really harmed is himself, because he's been duped out of money by an online fraudster.

Applying the stricter deontological criteria – that is, that adultery requires physical intimacy with another human – he is also in the clear. He never met or had sex with Annie/Ivan, thus did not risk getting 'her' pregnant or 'her' passing on an STD that he could have given to his wife. In short, he's only guilty of what generations of teenage boys have been doing several times a night from puberty onwards.

If, however, Martha applies virtue ethics to the situation – looking at Seth's intention in engaging in an online affair with Annie/Ivan and how this reflects on his character – she might take a different view. Regardless of the real sex of the person pretending to be Annie, Seth demonstrated his intention to cheat on his wife. Martha cannot be sure whether Seth would have actually met and had sex with Annie if she had been genuine and willing, but Martha is entitled to take a view. In several cases, cyber affairs have been accepted as grounds for divorce. When she finally quits laughing, what would you advise Martha to do about the wayward Seth?

ONLINE AFFAIRS ARE THE NEXT FRONTIER OF INFIDELITY. IS VIRTUAL CHEATING THE SAME AS REAL-TIME CHEATING, OR ARE WE PUNISHING THE GUILTY PARTY JUST FOR THINKING ABOUT BEING UNFAITHFUL?

069 GUILT-FREE ADULTERY

Madison is a happily married woman—mostly—but there are some areas of her relationship with Ted that leave something to be desired. After ten years of marriage, it's true to say that the magic has gone out of the couple's sex life. They rarely have sex, and when they do, it feels to Madison that they are both 'going through the motions', with Madison thinking about George Clooney (when she's not planning the menu for her next dinner party) before faking an orgasm, while Ted—well, she doesn't want to imagine what he might be thinking about…

They used to have such great sex for the first five years of their marriage. Then the kids came along, and Madison and Ted got so comfortable with one another that the fires of carnal passion were doused.

Madison decides to talk to her friend Ashley about her worries. Madison and Ashley went to university together, were married the same year,

THE INTERNET IS HAVING FAR-REACHING SOCIAL AND ETHICAL IMPACTS ON MANY ASPECTS OF LIFE. HOW IS IT TRANSFORMING REAL-TIME SEX?

and have similar marital issues between the sheets. 'It's amazing!' Ashley rhapsodises about her latest Internet discovery: an adultery website called UndercoverSins.com. 'The men are soooo hot! And it's soooo discreet!' Ashley explains that a profile on the site can be anonymous and is only visible to members. 'But what if Ted saw me?' Madison asks. 'The only way he'd be able to see you was if he'd signed up too.'

Joining an adultery website would provide Madison with a discreet way of being unfaithful. If it could save her marriage, is it worth the risk?

Guilt-free, shame-free?

In *The Chrysanthemum and the Sword* (1946) American anthropologist Ruth Benedict (1887–1948) made the interesting but oversimplified observation that while Japanese culture was based on shame, Western culture was based on guilt. One wonders what she would have made of the Internet – a medium whose anonymity at least allows its users shame-free real-time interactions. Are contemporary views of sexual immorality more dependent on whether you are found out than on your own conscience?

For better or worse

A rule utilitarian would most likely argue that adultery of any kind is usually wrong, while a strict utilitarian such as Jeremy Bentham might take a more nuanced view, wishing to weigh the potential harms (pain) against the potential benefits (pleasure). How likely is it that Madison's marriage will fail because the partners no longer fulfill one another sexually? If it does, it will hurt not only them but their children and families. On the other hand, if she is unfaithful and is found out, how likely is it to bring the marriage to an end? Or would the couple reach some kind of arrangement? A third outcome is that Madison has one or more affairs through the website and is no longer sexually frustrated, ensuring the survival of her marriage and, who knows, maybe even reinvigorating her sex life with Ted.

♋070 STAR-CROSSED CYBER LOVERS

Romeo has been going out with Juliet for a year now. Like many school kids, their romance is both an on- and offline affair. When they can't meet, they text, instant message and exchange and post photos on each other's social media accounts. To Lucy's mother, who grew up and got married before the digital media revolution, it is mystifying to learn that her daughter is in twenty-four-hour communication with most of her besties, and with Romeo, through one platform or another, wherever they are in the world. Even when they went to France for a two-week holiday, there was no pause in the steady exchange of photos, comments and sweet nothings, despite the distance.

When disaster strikes, it strikes in such an unexpected way that both sets of parents are completely unprepared. The lovers have had a terminal falling out—did Romeo catch Juliet with Mercutio, or was Romeo caught *in flagrante* with Rosalind? Whatever happened, it was bad, and the fallout is worse. Romeo starts sharing naked pictures that Juliet sent him, and she responds in kind. Soon the pictures are all over school, and they come to the attention of the head teacher, who calls the police. Both teens are charged with distributing child pornography, because of the nature of the pictures, and invasion of privacy because of the revenge-porn aspect of their subsequent distribution.

IN TERMS OF SEX AND SEXUAL MORES, THE INTERNET CAN HIGHLIGHT SOME NIGHTMARISH ETHICAL ISSUES, BUT JUST HOW BAD IS IT?

Tragedy of errors

The two previous dilemmas have explored several of the sexual issues raised by the Internet – dishonesty and exploitation – but the current dilemma adds two new problem areas for ethicists and lawyers: the consensual distribution of sexual images of minors, but by the minors themselves, and the redistribution of these images as 'revenge porn'.

In many states, it is currently the former that is treated much more seriously, because it is currently covered by legislation making child pornography illegal. Laws that were designed to deter and punish the non-consensual abuse of children by adults are now being used to prosecute minors who are creating and distributing sexual images of themselves, leading to their placement on the sex offenders register.

An issue that might be considered to be a much greater violation of privacy, revenge porn – the publication of intimate photographs for malicious reasons – when minors are not involved, is covered by the civil offences of tort and copyright violation.

The greatest incongruity, however, must be the equation of non-consensual child pornography produced by adults for other adults, and the consensual images exchanged privately between teenagers. Granted, Romeo and Juliet are not innocent, but should they be labelled sex offenders?

Bad and badder

The Internet's ethical blackspots include:
- dishonesty (fake profiles)
- breaches of human dignity (trolling)
- sexual exploitation and abuse (grooming)
- normalisation of criminal sexual acts
- Internet addiction
- childhood exposure to sexual adult practices
- creation of unrealistic expectations of sex and sexual partners.

SCIENTIFIC

'Science, as long as it limits itself to the descriptive study of the laws of nature, has no moral or ethical quality and this applies to the physical as well as the biological sciences.'

– Sir Ernst Boris Chain (1906–1979)

₀071 DAY-GLO MICE

It is the near future. A small boy goes into a very special kind of pet shop. He can barely contain his excitement. 'Are they ready?' he asks the kindly looking old man (which is actually the robotic interface of this automated shop). 'Hold your horses, sonny', the robot says in a folksy style. 'I'll just go round the back. I think they're ready.' The robot swivels around and retreats smoothly on tracks through an automatic door camouflaged by an antique beaded curtain.

The simulated old man reappears minutes later with an oblong grey container the size and appearance of a cardboard shoebox, which he places carefully on the counter in front of the boy. The robot touches a small switch on the side of the box, whose sides instantly become transparent. The box contains two mice. They look like two ordinary white albino mice until the robot dims the lights in the shop. In response, the mice begin to glow in a disconcerting display of electric shades of pink, blue, red and purple. The robot explains that the genes of several bioluminescent jellyfish give the mice their unusual ability.

'They're not dangerous?' a slightly worried mother asks.
'Quite harmless', the robot replies.
'They are fully grown, cannot
reproduce and have a life
expectancy of fourteen
months and ten days.'

OUR UNDERSTANDING
OF THE GENOMES OF
PLANTS AND ANIMALS WILL ALLOW US UNPRECEDENTED
FREEDOM TO ENGINEER ENTIRELY NEW LIFEFORMS. IS THIS
TO BE WELCOMED OR A STEP TOO FAR?

All creatures great and small

Essentially, what the shop in the scenario on the previous page is doing is breeding animate toys. But is that in any way different from the production of other 'toy' animal species we have produced already by conventional breeding techniques, such as miniature chihuahuas to fit in the handbags of the rich and vain, or wonderfully coloured koi carp for collectors? Is the difference that the chihuahua and koi could theoretically have happened 'naturally', however unlikely that might be, while there is no way a mouse could have interacted with a jellyfish to produce an entirely novel lifeform such as luminescent mice?

American philosopher and animal-rights activist Bernard Rollin (b. 1943) suggests that a suitable principle with which to regulate genetic engineering would be that genetically engineered organisms should be no worse off than the parent stock would be if they were not engineered.

We can try to apply this to our glow-in-the-dark mice scenario: Sadly, it is the role of the pet animals of small children to live short, pathetic lives that are often cut short when the child forgets about them or accidentally or intentionally kills them. The lives of wild mice are, if anything, shorter and more pathetic than those of domesticated mice, and as little is known about the lives of jellyfish, it is difficult to apply Rollin's principle in this situation.

'Like every human activity, biotechnology is open to wise and foolish uses. The profit motive, coupled with an uncritical acceptance of the notion that new technology is the main way to human advancement, often leads to hype and incautious applications.'
— **Stuart A. Newman (b. 1945)**

⸂072 SAVING ANIMALS

Case 1

A team of medical researchers is conducting a programme of animal testing on mice and non-human primates to study the progression of muscular dystrophy— an incurable muscle-weakening condition that kills many of its sufferers and leaves others severely disabled. Animal research, while it has not led to the discovery of a cure, has enabled researchers to develop a much better understanding of the disease, and therefore may one day lead to a cure. In order to study the condition, they have had to breed research animals that suffer from the disease. These animal subjects will suffer the same symptoms as human patients.

Case 2

Another team of researchers is studying a particularly debilitating and painful form of rheumatoid arthritis that affects children and young adults. However, the condition is not fatal and is episodic, and, though not curable, can usually be managed with painkilling drugs and physical therapy. As in Case 1, researchers have had to breed research animals that suffer from the disease, thereby causing them the same debilitating and painful episodes as human sufferers.

Case 3

A team is testing the safety and effectiveness of a revolutionary type of corrective surgery for visual defects. The research necessitates the removal of the natural lenses in the eyes of the test subjects and their replacement with new artificial lenses. The procedure may lead to great discomfort and possible blindness for the research animals.

WHILE YOU MIGHT BE ABLE TO JUSTIFY THE HARM CAUSED TO ANIMALS BY THE LIFESAVING TREATMENTS ANIMAL TESTING HAS MADE POSSIBLE, WHAT ABOUT TESTING THE LATEST SHAMPOOS AND COSMETICS?

Subjects-of-a-life

American philosopher Tom Regan uses Kantian principles to argue the case for animal rights, but whereas Kant would base his defence of human rights on rationality, Regan argues that a living being has moral rights, if it has a life that it itself values – that it is a 'subject-of-a-life'. Certain humans, after all, do not display rationality: babies, the seriously mentally impaired, and people in comas, yet we still grant them moral rights. If the valuing of one's own life is used to determine the value of a human or non-human being's existence, then neither a human nor an animal can be used as the means to an end.

Unlike Rollin (see previous dilemma), Regan does not believe that any being's moral rights are absolute. In the three cases given above, Case 1 might lead to lifesaving treatments; Case 2 might relieve great human suffering; but Case 3 is evaluating a treatment that is almost cosmetic in nature, as spectacles and other procedures already correct this particular defect. Which of the three cases, if any, do you think justifies harming or killing animals?

☙073 BEING HUMAN

A laboratory is conducting research that has the potential to provide an unlimited supply of viable human stem cells without the involvement of a human donor. This has vast implications in several key areas of medical research, including drug testing, and genetic and regenerative medicine.
In order to study the production of stem cells and also evaluate their viability, they are first incorporated into animal embryos, resulting in the creation of a living being with separate genetic material from its original parents and from humans: a human–nonhuman 'chimera'.

The first of our bioluminescent mice (see pp. 156–157) would have been a genetic chimera, that is, a mix of two animal genomes, whose creation raises animal-rights issues. But with a human–nonhuman chimera, one has to consider a whole other set of issues; namely, how human does the incorporation of human genetic material make the resulting entity? According to the legal regulation of this type

HUMANS AND ANIMALS CURRENTLY HAVE VERY DIFFERENT MORAL RIGHTS. STEM-CELL RESEARCH IS BLURRING THE LINE BETWEEN ANIMAL AND HUMAN, SO HOW HUMAN DO YOU HAVE TO BE, TO BE CONSIDERED FULLY HUMAN?

of research in most jurisdictions, it makes it human enough to make it illegal for these types of embryos to be implanted into a womb and allowed to grow to term.

This is not sci-fi: There is no danger that you would get a mouse or chicken with a tiny human face, consciousness and intelligence, but if allowed to grow to term and be born, you would get a mouse or a chicken with substantial human genetic material in every single one of its cells. Would eating this chicken or its eggs be the same as eating a human being?

Mix and match

American philosopher Robert Streiffer (b. 1970) outlines the five main ethical arguments raised by human–nonhuman chimeras:

- Unnaturalness: They violate the 'natural' boundaries between humans and animal species. However, 'naturalness' is difficult to define. We exchange genetic material with other species (with bacteria) and with other humans (between mother and fetus).
- Moral confusion: We employ different moral frameworks for humans and animals. The very existence of chimeric beings would cause a kind of moral confusion that will be damaging to society as a whole because so many of our ethical and legal principles are based on a clear difference in the distinction between human and animal.

- Borderline personhood: In the case of our nearest cousins, the great apes (chimps, orangutans and gorillas), their closeness to us and the 'personhood' we endow them with means that all chimeric research on them would be unethical.
- Human dignity: Creating a nonhuman being with human capacities is an affront to human dignity.
- Moral status framework: A human–nonhuman chimera cannot have the moral rights and status of an animal or of a human being. If it is an animal, it can be used in research and killed, but a human cannot be used in this way. Chimeric research itself denies the chimera human status and moral rights.

074 DRIVERLESS CAR CRASHES

It is the year 2030. Driverless cars are everywhere, and they're pretty much accepted as an ordinary part of the modern world. Of course, there are some old timers who still drive manual cars. You're 'driving' one evening after work, but instead of heading to your house in the burbs, you're meeting a friend for dinner downtown.

Normally, you stick to the freeway from your office to your house. The traffic – 99 percent driverless now – is smooth and problem-free. There used to be traffic jams on the freeway at peak times, but with driverless cars everything is optimised and jams and accidents are things of the past. You spend most of your drive time working, reading, watching TV or chatting with friends online. Tonight is no different, even though you're going into the city, where there are many more hazards: pedestrians, cyclists, rollerbladers and any number of other obstacles.

The car is constantly monitoring its surroundings – much more efficiently than a human driver could. There is a manual override on the car, but you wouldn't ever use it; taking over control would probably make things worse, and your insurance recommends that you leave the car on automatic to avoid any personal liability.

That's when the crash happens…

DRIVERLESS CARS MAY SOON BE COMMONPLACE ON OUR ROADS AND MOTORWAYS. IN THE VERY LIKELY EVENT OF A CRASH, THE CAR MIGHT HAVE TO CHOOSE WHO TO KILL. WILL IT BE YOU?

Accidents will happen

Even with driverless cars, crashes will happen. American philosopher Patrick Lin has put forward two scenarios involving a driverless car that illuminate possible ethical issues:

Crash 1: Eeny, meeny...
Your car has to crash into one of two neighbouring vehicles: an SUV or a much frailer hatchback. Both cars are carrying a mother and baby strapped into a child's seat. Which vehicle should the driverless car hit? If it hits the SUV, the passengers are much more likely to survive, but is that fair for the SUV driver? Would drivers start buying less solid cars so as to reduce their chances of getting hit?

Crash 2: Moral luck
In this scenario, the car has to pick between two motorbike riders: one is wearing a helmet, the other is not. If the car hits the one without the helmet, the chances are that he will be killed, while the rider with the helmet has a better chance of survival. This is a classic case of moral luck: The 'good' rider will be hit because he has been more responsible, while the 'bad' rider will escape because he has been reckless.

So what should the car do? Blow itself up, killing you rather than either rider?

Lin suggests getting around the problem by preventing the car from knowing certain facts and allowing it to pick at random, but this negates some of the clear advantages of driverless technology. In any case, insurance companies would probably not allow it.

'Seniors can keep their freedom even if they can't keep their car keys. And drunk and distracted driving? History.'
– **Per Liljas, *Time* magazine**

⚇075 I, DOCTOR

Imagine a future where automated systems (such as driverless cars) have been around for decades. But they are low-grade intelligence compared to the sophisticated AI (artificial intelligence) devices that are now being developed for a wide variety of applications. In addition to their usual applications in the workplace, they are now increasingly employed in life-and-death situations such as warfare and healthcare, where they are taking the place of clinicians as trauma doctors and surgeons.

As a result of the crash your driverless car was involved in (see previous dilemma), the person you hit is rushed to the nearest A&E with serious head injuries, multiple bone fractures and internal bleeding. His chances of survival are limited, and the human A&E doctors, fearing malpractice lawsuits if he dies or is permanently impaired, have decided to entrust his care to the A&E's medbot. Rather than a George-Clooney-lookalike android, the medbot is a suite of instruments controlled by a central processor within an operating theatre.

Like any other doctor, the medical robot will be asked to make life-and-death decisions about whether to attempt a risky procedure or decide not to perform it, by making a judgement about what would be best for the patient (based on the four ethical principles outlined on p. 109).

SCI-FI AUTHOR ISAAC ASIMOV (1920–1992) FIRST PROPOSED THE THREE LAWS OF ROBOTICS TO WHICH A ROBOT MUST CONFORM. COULD THEY EVER BE ENFORCED IN REAL-WORLD SITUATIONS?

The Three Laws of Robotics

We would expect that such a robot would have a high degree of autonomy, but would also have to be constrained in its behaviour by fail-safes. Among these, the most famous are Asimov's Three Laws of Robotics:

1. A robot may not injure a human being or, through inaction, allow a human being to come to harm.
2. A robot must obey the orders given to it by human beings, except where such orders would conflict with the First Law.
3. A robot must protect its own existence as long as such protection does not conflict with the First or Second Laws.

As Asimov was writing fiction not real robot ethics, these laws do not work in practice. The medbot is likely to break the first law on a daily basis, in cases when the mathematical odds of a patient being helped or harmed by a procedure are so well-balanced that it would be impossible to choose, but doing nothing is not an option. It would also encounter situations when the laws would come into conflict, causing a meltdown. As we saw in the drone and battlefield-robot dilemmas, to be fully autonomous a robot would have to work out its own ethical positions. There is no guarantee that it would not create a system of ethics completely at odds with our own.

If our ethical systems are based on our empathy with fellow human beings, combined with enlightened self-interest, in that we want to be treated as we ourselves treat others, what would motivate a non-human AI to do the same?

'Why give a robot an order to obey orders – why aren't the original orders enough? Why command a robot not to do harm – wouldn't it be easier never to command it to do harm in the first place?'
– **Steven Pinker (b. 1954)**

⸮076 ROBOT RAPE

In the near future, a number of corporations are offering bespoke lifelike androids as personal bedroom companions (PBC). These are more than just sophisticated dolls. In addition to their external appearance, the latest generation of PBCs can be designed with the customer's chosen personality traits. Most customers want 'standard' models in terms of appearance and personality, though, of course, there is a great deal of variety. But there are also customers with 'special' requests for non-standard models. These customers are referred to an offshore company in East Asia, where their orders can be treated with much greater discretion. Let's look at three of these non-standard orders:

Order 1: The masterful man

Sally has always liked older, masterful men. A fan of nineteenth-century fiction, she imagines herself pursued by a Mr Darcy, who takes her forcibly, and when she refuses his advances, he thrashes her with his riding crop until she obeys his every whim. Essentially, she is playing out domestic violence and rape fantasies with her robot lover. In most jurisdictions, non-consensual treatment of this kind by a human being would be classed as rape and assault.

Order 2: Lolita

Charles has always had a thing about young girls and boys. He has ordered seven-year-old twins, one male, one female, which he intends to 'abuse' and have sex with. He wants them to be mentally as close to real children as possible.

Order 3: The victim

Bill has ordered a classic streetwalker robot. He intends to simulate paying her for sex, public sex and also forced sex. Essentially, he wants a robot to degrade, humiliate and rape.

CONSIDERING THE PACE OF AI DEVELOPMENT, THE POSSIBILITY OF SEX WITH A SENTIENT ROBOT CANNOT BE FAR AWAY. WOULD LAWS ON SEXUAL CRIME APPLY TO ROBOTS? OR IS AN INTELLIGENT MACHINE ALWAYS JUST A MACHINE?

Ghost in the machine

If these robots were fully autonomous, they would be sentient, and therefore moral beings in their own right, which according to Kant, should not be used as a means to another's ends. But let's set that aside and say they are only partly autonomous. Hence Mr Darcy can only behave in the way Sally wants. If she is injured or killed, who is to blame? The robot, the manufacturer or Sally?

In the other two orders, it is the customer who is doing the abusing. Given that these are not sentient robots, there are no issues of consent or exploitation – not unless you can abuse an inanimate object. But Order 2 might present an issue for ethicists and lawmakers. The robots are not children, but they are accurate representations of children and more 'alive' than photographs or video clips. If it is a crime to view child pornography, should reenacting it with a robot also be a crime? In one sense, the two actions are analogous. The difference is that in child porn involving real children, harm has been done to the children in its production. The viewer is an accessory to a crime. But in the case of a robot, there is no human victim.

⚬077 THE BEST WE CAN BE

Kenneth and Barbara's 'designer babies' (see pp. 120–121), Ken and Barbie, have grown up and are now at school. The couple wanted their son Ken to have an above-average ability at sport and they opted for their daughter Barbie to be academically gifted. But genetic engineering, as their counsellor at Perfect Baby, Inc., explained, is still not an exact science. Although the genes that control physical appearance and mental capacities are known, their expression in the real world is not straightforward: The environment still has a very large effect on how a child develops.

In Ken's case, he is tall for his age and he will probably reach his target height of 190 cm as an adult, but he has not got the muscle bulk or stamina that he needs to excel at sport. Meanwhile, Barbie, who is very bright, has problems concentrating on one thing for any length of time, meaning that though she has the potential to succeed academically, her actual performance is below par. Adding to the problem is the fact that most of the children at Ken and Barbie's school are also the product of genetic engineering, and so the overall average has been lifted several notches.

Kenneth and Barbara are advised to go to Life Enhanced, Inc., a company offering both physical and cognitive enhancements. Ken would be given a cocktail of drugs that would bulk him out and improve his stamina and Barbie would be given drugs that increase her concentration span and boost her intelligence.

'Many of the cognitive enhancement drugs serve to increase focus and concentration. But 'letting your mind wander' is very often an important part of the creative process.'
– Jamais Cascio (b. 1966)

To dope or not to dope

As the 2016 scandal around the Russian Olympic team (among others) demonstrated, performance-enhancing drugs are already with us in the world of elite sports, as well as among the most determined of amateur athletes and gym-goers, who hope to improve their physiques using steroids and human growth hormone. Both the professional and amateur use of doping is currently illegal and often dangerous to users. Similarly, drugs such as Ritalin, which is used therapeutically for ADHD, are used illicitly by students hoping to improve academic performance.

It is possible to foresee a time when drugs with even more potent effects will be developed, boosting the abilities of those who can afford them. As with the creation of 'designer babies', there is a basic equity argument, if only the rich are able to afford to enhance themselves and their offspring.

On the other hand, one could argue that enhancement is what being human is all about. Without technological and cultural enhancements, we would still be living in the trees picking lice off one another. If the main argument against performance-enhancing technologies is that they are unnatural, what about schooling, aspirin and reading glasses? If everyone were able to benefit from the same enhancements (i.e., if all sportsmen doped), would that make enhancements socially acceptable?

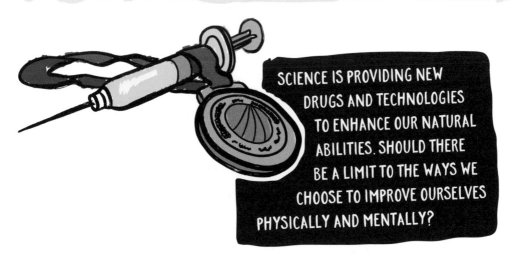

SCIENCE IS PROVIDING NEW DRUGS AND TECHNOLOGIES TO ENHANCE OUR NATURAL ABILITIES. SHOULD THERE BE A LIMIT TO THE WAYS WE CHOOSE TO IMPROVE OURSELVES PHYSICALLY AND MENTALLY?

ஃ078 PURE KNOWLEDGE

The ever-upwardly-mobile Sally has left the Department for Collective Apologies (see pp. 100–101), and is now in charge of a committee looking into government funding of scientific research – a spend that amounts to tens of billions of pounds a year. This is money that could be spent on medical research, such as finding cures for cancer. Sally has been asked to come up with a list of programmes to slim down or shut down. But she hasn't been given very much guidance as to what types of research, and in what disciplines, she should be targeting.

To help her decide, she has asked the heads of several government-backed agencies and research programmes to justify the funding they receive. This justification should not be based purely on financial returns (as several are unlikely to come up with any commercial applications and would be unfairly disadvantaged), but on the moral case for the continuation of their funding. The first of four multi-volume justifications lands on her desk and threatens to crush it under its weight. Here are the edited versions Sally comes up with:

MANNED SPACE EXPLORATION, COSMOLOGY AND THE SEARCH FOR EXOPLANETS ARE ALL EXAMPLES OF SCIENTIFIC PROJECTS THAT HAVE NO TANGIBLE BENEFITS. DOES THAT MAKE THEM IMMORAL?

Submission 1: Manned space exploration

(Specifically, the exploration of celestial bodies within the solar system and beyond, rather than any practical applications of space technology.)

Manned exploration is what has driven the human race forward socially, culturally and intellectually. It could be argued that the prehistoric human migration out of Africa is what created the human race. To abandon manned exploration of space would be to belittle the human race and accept that we are no longer able to develop.

Submission 2: Cosmology

(Investigations about the nature of the universe, how it began and will end, and the study of distant astronomical bodies such as pulsars, quasars and black holes.)

New ways of understanding the nature of the universe creates paradigm shifts in our thinking that have transformative effects in all aspects of human life. For example, Albert Einstein's (1879–1955) theories of special and general relativity had no practical applications in 1905, and several were only proved experimentally many years after his death, but they have shaped the modern world.

Submission 3: Search for exoplanets

(The search for planets outside our solar system, which we may never be able to visit.)

This may answer the greatest question of all: are we alone? Is life unique to the Earth or does it fill the universe? The discovery of extraterrestrial life will forever transform our understanding of ourselves and our place in the universe. The discovery of sentient intelligent life on one of these planets would be even more significant.

These types of science research projects cannot create better therapies to cure cancer or better engineering technologies to produce energy, but they help define what it is to be human, and show us there is no limit to what humans can aspire to. In short, they show us the people we could become.

♋079 ARTIFICIAL WOMBS

We are now several generations on from Kenneth and Barbara's designer babies (pp. 120–121). In this brave new world, all embryos are fertilised *in vitro* (in the lab), rigorously screened for any impairment, and genetically engineered to maximise their physical and mental potential, slow down the ageing process, and increase their expectancy to an average age of 250. Increased lifespans mean that the population has to be carefully controlled so that numbers do not exceed resources.

K1203-X and B3029-Y are two individuals considered by the Directorate of Population to have optimum genotypes whose combination would enhance the human gene pool. They have been offered the rare privilege of providing gametes (ovum and sperm) for the creation of a new embryo. Once fertilised, screened and enhanced, the embryo will be implanted in an artificial womb in a gestation centre.

The two individuals have the choice of remaining anonymous or meeting the other donor; they can also choose to take some responsibility for the child as its official 'parent', or to assign it to the care of the Directorate of Education. Given these reproductive arrangements, there is no necessity for marriage or any other kind of relationship between the parents. They may wish to meet and interact, but once they have agreed to donate their gametes, their relationship, or lack of one, will not affect the future of the embryo, which will grow to term whatever they decide.

Is this a eugenics nightmare or the sensible shape of things to come?

AFTER IN-VITRO FERTILISATION, IS THE NEXT STAGE OF HUMAN REPRODUCTION EX-UTERO GESTATION? HOW WOULD THAT CHANGE THE NATURE OF PARENTING?

Happy families

Before the existence of reliable contraception and legal abortion, reproductive arrangements within a heterosexual nuclear family meant that the wife had to give up her autonomy and self-ownership to the husband and, by implication, that of the embryo she carried. The current situation means that the mother has gained autonomy but the embryo has lost protection, if the mother chooses to terminate the pregnancy. In the scenario above, changes in reproductive technology have effectively abolished the nuclear family, which has no significant legal, social or moral functions. This does not mean that people would not choose to procreate naturally, but how many would if they were no longer obliged to do so by biology?

Pro-life

Although pro-life supporters may be horrified by the idea of an artificial womb, it actually ensures the victory of their cause. There would no longer be any unplanned, unwanted children. Once implanted into the artificial womb, the child would become fully autonomous. It might not be deemed to have personhood until it was born, but it would no longer be dependent on the health or goodwill of another human being for its survival.

Who gets control?

Artificial gestation removes the automatic presumption that the biological parents would have control of the embryo and future child. In the above scenario the state gets control, but it could also be a private corporation or a social group in charge of reproduction.

NATURAL
WORLD

'An understanding of the natural world and what's in it is a source of not only a great curiosity but great fulfillment.'
– David Attenborough (b. 1926)

080 HUMANS FIRST

The 'visitors' are ushered into a specially designed chamber with an atmosphere quite different from Earth's. Once inside, they can remove their cumbersome breathing apparatus and take their places at the conference table that extends through a glass partition into a room where a human delegation is already seated. The theme of today's conference is the biosphere of each planet.

The visitors open the discussion with a description of the biosphere of their own world. When the humans reply, they hit a snag in translation. The aliens don't understand the distinction between 'human' and 'animal', as their own languages and cultures don't make a distinction between two distinct classes of living beings. 'But humans are animals?' an alien asks. It goes on, 'You are one group descended from a common ancestor 3.5 billion years ago. Are you not a continuum of lifeforms?'

IF YOU TAKE IT FOR GRANTED THAT HUMANS ARE FUNDAMENTALLY DIFFERENT FROM ANIMALS, YOU COULD BE ACCUSED OF 'SPECIESISM'. CAN THIS NEW '-ISM' REALLY BE EQUATED WITH RACISM AND SEXISM?

There is a discussion on the human side, trying to explain the complex relationship between humans and animals since the evolution of *Homo sapiens*, including the farming of animals for food. The aliens are incredulous and horrified. 'You eat your fellow creatures?' The aliens extract nutrients from their atmosphere, so they do not raise crops or farm animals for food. 'Do you eat other humans?' one asks. 'No, no', a human replies. 'Only non-human animals. And then only certain species.'

If you were an alien, would you be worried about the implications for your own treatment by humans?

Them and us

British animal-rights advocate Richard Ryder (b. 1940) came up with the idea of 'speciesism', equating the exploitation of animals with racism and sexism. According to Ryder and Australian philosopher Peter Singer, who popularised the concept, speciesism discriminates against all non-human beings, because they belong to the class 'animals', as opposed to the distinct class of 'humans', which are treated morally in completely different ways: You can own animals, you can kill them when they get sick, you can perform experiments on them, and, of course, you can eat them.

The human–animal divide is a historical construct with its roots in religious conceptions of man not just as the top animal, but as a distinct class of being. Animal studies have gradually chipped away at the difference between human and animals: symbolic communication, tool use, emotion, self-awareness, memory, and awareness of death have been tentatively identified in a number of animal species.

Critics counter that there is no equivalence between racism and sexism and speciesism because there is a clear difference between humans and animals, while race and gender are not valid criteria to differentiate between humans. Furthermore, the civil-rights and feminist movements were initiated and prosecuted by African Americans and women, who were aware of the injustices perpetrated against them and demanded redress. We cannot know what an animal thinks about its life – or even if it can think about its life at all.

₀₈₁ 081 DEAD AS A DODO

It is the seventeenth century. Jan van Huis, a settler from the small Dutch colony on the island of Mauritius, is out hunting. A large flightless bird the size of a goose waddles into view. Jan fires a shot with his musket, killing the dodo. The colonists would not touch the flesh of the bird unless they were starving. Fortunately, there are plenty of wild pigs on the island, which is what Jan is really after.

Jan doesn't know it, but he has shot the last female dodo of breeding age. A small number of male birds will survive for another few years, and when they die, the species will be officially extinct. It has taken about eighty years from the arrival of the Dutch until the eradication of the harmless dodo, partly through hunting but mainly from the depredations of invasive species such dogs, cats, rats and pigs that the settlers brought with them. Unconcerned, Jan continues his hunt in search of more palatable prey.

Evolving from a flying pigeon into the flightless dodo on an island without predators, the bird did not stand a chance when the world's apex predator – humans – arrived.

THE FLIGHTLESS DODO IS THE BEST-KNOWN CASE OF EXTINCTION DIRECTLY ATTRIBUTABLE TO HUMAN ACTIVITY. BUT WHY SHOULD WE CARE IF WE LOSE A FEW SPECIES BY THE BIOLOGICAL WAYSIDE?

Conservation is self-preservation

American biologist Michael Soulé (b. 1936), the leading advocate of 'conservation biology', argues that all species have a role to play in the preservation of our fragile biosphere. He has written: 'The worth of nature is beyond question and our obligation to minimise its gratuitous degradation is no less'. For Soulé, even the eradication of one species threatens the whole, and is deeply immoral and against humanity's long-term interests.

The Rapa Nui analogy

Rapa Nui, also known as Easter Island, is a prime lesson in how not to manage an ecosystem. It was settled during the first millennium by Polynesian colonists, who sailed up to 2,000 miles (3,200 km) to reach what was then a fertile, forested island, with a diverse fauna and flora. It took the Rapa Nui five or six centuries to exhaust the island's natural resources, depleting its soils so that their agriculture failed and cutting down most of the trees, preventing them from building boats to migrate to a new home. Instead of trying to slow or prevent the impending ecological catastrophe, they fought a series of destructive wars – it all sounds dreadfully familiar, doesn't it?

'The prime motive of science is not to control the universe but to appreciate it more fully. It is a huge privilege to live on Earth and to share it with so many goodly and fantastical creatures.'

– **Colin Tudge (b. 1943)**

082 HUNTING BAN

Case 1: Subsistence hunting

For most of prehistory humans lived as nomadic hunter-gatherers, travelling in small bands and living off the land and hunting sustainably, taking just enough to satisfy their needs – such is the romanticised version of prehistoric hunting. The reality is a little more nuanced. As humanity spread across the world, its progress was associated with the extinction of all large animal species known as megafauna.

Modern subsistence hunting, however, that takes common species that are not endangered and that might otherwise damage crops or degrade the environment, can be justified from a consequentialist position, on the grounds that killing the animals will prevent this damage.

Case 2: Cultural hunting

Hunting can also be connected to religious practices and rites of passage. Among certain peoples in antiquity, and in Africa until the present day, the lion hunt was an important ritual and a rite of passage into manhood. Ritual lion hunts also served to protect herds of domesticated animals by reducing the number of predators.

Although we should have sympathy towards long-established cultural practices, this does not extend to allowing the hunting of protected or endangered species.

ANIMAL-RIGHTS ACTIVISTS ARGUE FOR A TOTAL BAN ON HUNTING ON THE GROUNDS OF CONSERVATION AND ANIMAL CRUELTY. BUT ARE ALL FORMS OF HUNTING EQUALLY WASTEFUL AND CRUEL?

Case 3: Therapeutic hunting

In an unbalanced ecological system where the apex predators have been removed, prey species will multiply, further damaging the environment. Limiting the number of certain species through therapeutic hunting restores the ecological balance, improving the lives of the remaining animals.

As with controlled subsistence hunting, a strong consequentialist case can be made for therapeutic hunting.

Case 4: Sport hunting

A wealthy professional man travels to Africa and pays a large amount of money to kill a lion purely for sport. The lion may have been bred in captivity, and rather than being the terrifying 'king of the jungle' it is a sitting duck for any passing shot.

Of the four types of hunting described here, it surely is the most morally repugnant. However, again, the situation is little more nuanced. In the poorer countries of the world that have the greatest concentrations of wildlife, the income generated by sport-hunting pays for overall conservation efforts. Without the funds provided by hunting, the land would be cleared and given over to cash crops or livestock. Paradoxically, the most reprehensible form of hunting may also be the most useful from a conservation standpoint.

Natural-born killers

Most wild animals are not hunted and killed by humans but by animal predators. Does the logic of animal rights mean that a lion that kills and eats a zebra is a first-degree murderer? That would be an interesting trial to sit in on – as long as the defendant refrained from eating the judge and jury!

Animals, however, are not free moral agents who understand the difference between right and wrong. An animal cannot tell right from wrong, and cannot willfully violate the rights of another animal. Therefore, an animal cannot commit murder.

083 GOING VEGGIE

The alien visitors that we encountered earlier (see pp. 176–177) are fascinated by human–animal interactions, especially our raising of other living beings to eat as food – something that the aliens do not need to do in their world. After a visit to a cattle ranch, an alien visitor discusses what it has seen with its human guide.

'The large herbivores you call cattle will reach maturity and then be killed and their flesh eaten by humans', says the visitor. 'They are bred for that purpose', the human explains. 'They would not exist otherwise.' 'But there are other animals on the ranch', the visitor goes on. 'The rancher's family owns dogs and cats. Do they get eaten too?' 'No', the human replies, explaining

Animals rights

Animal-rights advocate Peter Singer would agree with the alien visitor that our attitude to animal rights is confused in the extreme. The distinction we make between livestock, pets, vermin and wild animals is based on purely subjective categories that vary with place and time. Although we protect many animals from unnecessary cruelty, what greater cruelty could there be than raising them for slaughter?

If, as Singer argues, animal do have rights, then their most important right is not to be used as the culinary ends of humans. The logical conclusion of this position is that we should all become vegetarians, if not vegans, as surely the exploitation of animals for their products, wool, milk, eggs, etc., is also a breach of their rights. One problem with this approach is the issue of where we should draw the line between animals we must respect and those we can kill with moral impunity: Do we draw the line at higher mammals, or extend it to birds, reptiles and fish? What about insects and microbial life?

that they are pets. Finally, the visitor asks about the rats and mice that live in proximity with both humans and animals. The human guide explains the notion of vermin.

'Let me see if I have understood', the visitor begins. 'You kill cattle and eat them and that is OK; you do not kill or eat pets because you are in affective relationships with them; you kill vermin but do not eat them because that would be repugnant to you. But all are higher mammals who can feel pain and have a degree of sentience. Why do you treat them so differently?'

HUMANS ARE THE WORLD'S APEX PREDATOR, BUT UNLIKE BIG CATS AND WOLVES, WE ARE ALSO MORAL BEINGS. DOES THAT MEAN IT'S TIME WE GAVE UP RAISING ANIMALS TO KILL AND EAT THEM?

Animal consequences

The consequentialist case for vegetarianism can also be made with the argument that abstaining from meat and switching to a diet rich in vegetable protein would immediately increase the available food supply for humans, thereby solving the problem of world hunger at a stroke. Livestock rearing is not only extremely costly in terms of land and resources, it's also a significant producer of greenhouse gases. If livestock farming was discontinued and replaced by the cultivation of high-protein vegetable produce such as maize, pulses, rice and cereals, we might be well on the way to tackling global poverty and climate change.

084 CARBON LETOUT CLAUSE

The 15 April, 1912, the North Atlantic. In this hitherto undocumented incident in the sinking of the RMS *Titanic*, three people have managed to get to a lifeboat and escape the wreck of the great liner, but they have become separated from the other lifeboats and have no oars to propel themselves. On board are a wealthy society lady, a passenger in first class, dressed in a fur coat, and who is wearing most of her collection of fine jewels; a rather dour looking Presbyterian minister, dressed soberly in a winter coat; and a stoker who managed to escape the flooding of the engine room, but who is inappropriately dressed for the chilly North-Atlantic early morning.

But sartorial matters are not the passengers' main concern, because their lifeboat has been damaged and is taking in water. Fortunately, there are three buckets in the lifeboat that they can use to bail the water out. The seepage is slow but steady, and as they have no way of repairing the damage, they must keep the water down to a certain level in order to keep the boat afloat. The minister has worked out that if the water reaches the depth of two feet, they will have reached their tipping point, and no matter how much they bail, they won't be able to save the lifeboat.

Despite the admonitions and warnings of the minister, the society lady has decided that she won't bail out water, and she is paying the stoker to work twice as hard. So far, his valiant efforts have managed to keep the water just shy of two feet, but for how much longer?

Carbon tradeoffs

Carbon trading allows the world's richer, developed countries to continue producing more than their fair share of emissions by 'buying' the unused emissions quotas of poorer, less developed countries. Supporters of the system argue that the market is the most efficient mechanism to get the world to its low-carbon future, avoiding the drastic cuts in the living standards of the developed world that would otherwise be necessary. The transfer of funds will enable developing countries to invest in more sustainable technological development, thereby reducing their emissions even further. The tradeoff, however, is that the poorer countries have to accept a slower pace of development and lower living standards to sustain those of the richer countries, at least until the problem is solved for good.

Now, that is all fine and rosy if carbon trading is reducing worldwide carbon emissions at the rate needed to slow down global warming and climate change. Unfortunately, it isn't, and we have either reached the critical tipping point or are about to. In terms of the analogy, the minister and stoker on their own cannot bail out enough water, and the society lady will have to join in if the boat is to stay afloat.

CARBON TRADING IS A TEMPORARY MEASURE DESIGNED TO ENABLE DEVELOPED ECONOMIES TO REACH THEIR CARBON-REDUCTION TARGETS WITHOUT REDUCING THEIR CARBON OUTPUT. SO DOES IT GIVE RICH COUNTRIES A MEANS TO EVADE THEIR RESPONSIBILITIES?

085 SAVING THE EARTH

It is the twenty-second century. The Earth has managed to survive the previous century's carbon crisis, but only just. The population of the planet is ten billion and climbing. Most humans now live crowded into megacities, because all the remaining land needs to be given over to agricultural production, which is only just managing to keep up with population growth. Through strict rationing and ever more repressive social control measures, the world government is succeeding in keeping some semblance of order.

Humanity's only hope is to forge out into space, mining the other planets and moons of the solar system for resources and seeking new homes for Earth's burgeoning population. Scientists have identified Earth-like planets in neighbouring solar systems, but the technology to transport the billions who need to leave the Earth in order for human society to survive still does not exist. What happens if, this time, technology fails to provide a solution?

Are we doomed to be forever arguing over who has to pay for what, letting the planetary environment degrade to such a point that no one can survive?

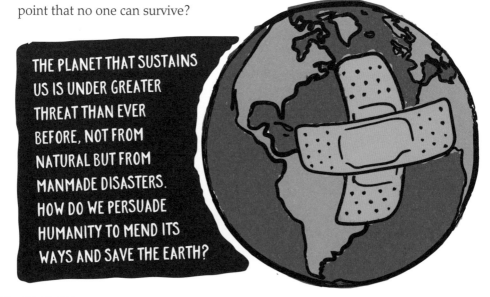

THE PLANET THAT SUSTAINS
US IS UNDER GREATER
THREAT THAN EVER
BEFORE, NOT FROM
NATURAL BUT FROM
MANMADE DISASTERS.
HOW DO WE PERSUADE
HUMANITY TO MEND ITS
WAYS AND SAVE THE EARTH?

Deep ecology

Ever since the birth of the environmental movement in the 1970s, there has been a clear utilitarian case for international co-operation to resolve issues of pollution, climate change and the equitable distribution of available resources. Yet, throughout most of the late twentieth and early twenty-first centuries, humanity attempted to use market mechanisms to solve the climate, population and resource crises, and the planet was saved in extremis by a series of fortuitous technological breaks.

In the late twentieth century, Danish philosopher Arne Næss (1912–2009) coined the term 'deep ecology' to describe the new understanding of the natural environment that he believed would enable humanity to survive in the long term. He contrasted it with the pragmatic utilitarian 'shallow ecology' adopted by national governments, international bodies, and multinational corporations. Shallow ecology values the environment only in terms of its instrumental usefulness to humans; deep ecology, in contrast, claims that the whole environment and all its component parts, human and non-human, animate and inanimate, have their own intrinsic value, and that the survival of the whole is a function of the survival of its parts. Deep ecology can be summarised in the three following ideas:

- The integrity and diversity of the environment have a value independent of human needs. They are prerequisite to the survival of both the environment and humanity.
- The human impact on the environment is far too great. The way to lessen this impact is to reduce the human population to a more sustainable level.
- In addition to reducing their numbers, humans have to transform the way they live, so as to prevent further degradation of the environment and allow for its recovery.

LIFE AND DEATH

'It is our choices ... that show what we truly are, far more than our abilities.'
– J. K. Rowling

☙086 THE OVERCROWDED LIFEBOAT

You are the captain of the ship that sank after a collision with an iceberg in the North Atlantic (see p. 184). It went down so fast that a distress call could not be sent out. No one knows that the ship has been lost or its precise location. Therefore, you have little hope of imminent rescue. The lifeboat has space and provisions for fifteen survivors but now holds thirty, consisting of fifteen crew members and fifteen passengers. To make matters worse, a storm is brewing and as the sea gets rougher, water laps over the gunwales of the boat.

The only way the boat can stay afloat is if at least a dozen passengers are thrown overboard. The waters of the North Atlantic at this time of year are freezing and anyone cast into the sea will die in minutes. The lifeboat is not motorised and needs strong, experienced rowers if it is to survive the coming storm. On board are the crew, both male and female, ranging in age from twenty to forty, with you the eldest at fifty-five; among the passengers, there are seven adult men, ranging in age from eighteen to seventy-five, a seven-year-old boy, six women, ranging in age from twenty-five to eighty, and three girls of five, seven and twelve.

You only have a matter of minutes to make your decision. What do you do?

YOU ARE THE CAPTAIN OF AN OVERCROWDED LIFEBOAT. DO YOU THROW ANYONE OVERBOARD? AND IF SO, WHY?

Hope for the best

You could ask for altruistic volunteers to go overboard. There are many historical examples of this kind of behaviour in similar situations: During the sinking of RMS *Titanic* in similar circumstances, many male passengers and crew sacrificed their lives so that women and children could be saved. However, *Titanic* took two hours to sink and you only have minutes. And today, in these more selfish times, would anyone sacrifice themselves for the sake of others?

The needs of the many

If you were a utilitarian, you could reason that if you did nothing or waited for volunteers, the boat would be swamped and everyone would die. Similarly, if you were to draw lots, the weak might survive, also dooming the lifeboat. Therefore, in order to save as many lives as possible and ensure the survival of the boat, you should sacrifice the twelve least able among the survivors, including the elderly, the children, the injured, the disabled or those too weak to be of any use rowing.

The real story

The *William Brown* hit an iceberg in the North Atlantic in 1841, and the seamen in charge of the lifeboat were faced with this dilemma for real. They decided to force fourteen adult passengers overboard. After their rescue, the only member of the crew who could be found was put on trial for murder, but was convicted of manslaughter, paying a fine of $20 and spending six months in jail.

DEAD OR ALIVE

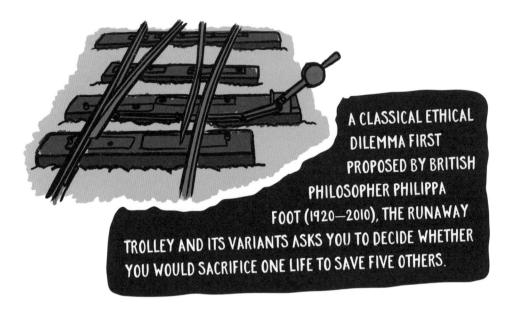

A CLASSICAL ETHICAL DILEMMA FIRST PROPOSED BY BRITISH PHILOSOPHER PHILIPPA FOOT (1920—2010), THE RUNAWAY TROLLEY AND ITS VARIANTS ASKS YOU TO DECIDE WHETHER YOU WOULD SACRIFICE ONE LIFE TO SAVE FIVE OTHERS.

087 THE RUNAWAY TROLLEY

You are standing overlooking a railway track that branches off into two lines. Some evil entity, wishing to test human morality, has tied five people to the main track and one person to the side track. You are next to the lever that can alter the trajectory of the train from one line to the other. You hear the sound of an approaching driverless trolley car that is barrelling down the track. There is no way of stopping the trolley car. You are faced with the choice of doing nothing and letting the trolley hit five people or diverting it onto the side track and killing one. Time is fast running out. What do you do?

Now imagine that you have been joined by a bunch of philosophers, who just happened to be on their departmental picnic in the same spot. The consequentialist will urge you to pull the lever: saving five lives must outweigh the regrettable loss of one. The deontologist might counter that by pulling the lever, you will immediately put yourself in the wrong by taking part in an immoral act – the taking of human life. Your best option is to do nothing. 'No, no, no!' says another philosopher. 'You have a moral obligation to act. I can tell you're a good person', she says, 'so your bad action will be justified by its good intention'.

088 THE FAT MAN

Judith Thomson (from the violinist dilemma, pp. 114–115) suggested this variant of the runaway trolley. In this case, you are standing on a bridge overlooking a single track. The five people are tied on the line as before, with a runaway trolley out of control careering towards them. The only way to stop the trolley is to throw something heavy in front of it. Unfortunately, the only thing at hand on the bridge that might do the trick is a very obese gentleman, who is helpfully leaning over the bridge parapet looking at the oncoming train.

In the classic version of the problem, you do not intend to harm any of the people on the track, but in Thomson's variant you have to decide whether to kill one person to save the lives of five others. How does this affect your decision? Would it help if the man was gloating about what was about to happen?

The philosophers can deploy the same arguments as before. And you can invoke the rule of double effect: You foresaw but did not intend the death of one person in order to save five lives.

089 THE MAN IN THE HAMMOCK

American philosopher Peter K. Unger (b. 1942) put forward a variant in which, in order to save the lives of the five people tied to the track, you have to derail the trolley car, killing an innocent bystander who is asleep in a hammock just below the tracks.

Does the fact that the man is a blameless bystander with no involvement in the problem affect your decision?

⸘090 THE CRUELEST CUT

You and your family find yourself in a situation that would be every parent's nightmare. You are part of a group of refugees fleeing from ruthless paramilitary militiamen, who you know will shoot you on sight. You run from hiding place to hiding place, attempting to reach the safety of your own army's lines, but they are still several miles away across hostile territory patrolled by the enemy.

Your three-month-old son is hungry, cold and terrified. Your wife has managed to keep him quiet until now, but he is getting more and more upset and noisier. You clamp your hand over his face to try to stifle his cries, but you risk suffocating him. Crouching inside the ruins of a bombed-out house, you hear the sound of approaching vehicles – the pickups the militiamen drive around in. Your baby begins to cry, threatening to give away your hiding place.

Hobson's choices

An Internet poll about the crying baby dilemma reported that sixty percent of respondents would suffocate the baby before he gave everyone away. Their consequentialist logic was irreproachable, as if the baby gave the group away, it would die with the rest. Therefore, sacrificing one life to save many more is a tradeoff that a majority of people would make.

Of the remaining forty percent, a proportion would refuse to kill an innocent child on the deontological grounds that it is always wrong, even at the near-certainty of losing their own life. Another group refused to decide, again condemning themselves to death, and a third group tried to find a way out of the dilemma, suggesting that they would prevent the child from crying by forcing his mouth shut, while trying not to suffocate him.

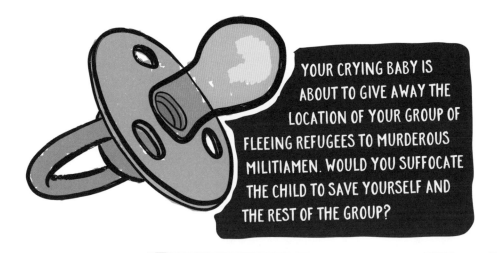

YOUR CRYING BABY IS ABOUT TO GIVE AWAY THE LOCATION OF YOUR GROUP OF FLEEING REFUGEES TO MURDEROUS MILITIAMEN. WOULD YOU SUFFOCATE THE CHILD TO SAVE YOURSELF AND THE REST OF THE GROUP?

Alternatives

Perhaps, though, there are other solutions to the dilemma.

Alternative 1:

You could split up the group, so that even if the baby did cry out and give your position away, at least the others might have a chance of getting away while the militiamen massacred you.

Alternative 2:

You could abandon the baby. It would probably start crying and attract the militiamen who might kill it, but then they might not. They might look after it or leave it to die, after which it might be found by a she-wolf and raised as a feral child (stranger things have happened). In either case, at least you would be spared the killing of your own baby son, and would have increased the chances of the whole group surviving.

Alternative 3:

You could make a run for it with the baby, leading the militiamen away from your wife and other children. By your altruistic sacrifice, you may save the rest of the group, and if you're a good runner you might even evade pursuit and survive yourself.

⅋091 PRISONER'S DILEMMA

Two close friends, Nate and Danny, hold up a newsagent late one night. The shopkeeper decides to be a hero and pulls a gun on the robbers, who are used to their victims holding up their hands and opening the till while begging them not to shoot. Panicking, they both fire their guns once, and the man goes down. As bad luck would have it, just as they are making their getaway, two squad cars pull up for their regular coffee and donut break. Outnumbered and cornered, the two criminals drop their guns and surrender.

The CCTV, the ballistics evidence and the testimony of the cops means it's an open-and-shut case. But the police have a problem: One gun fired the fatal shot, killing the shopkeeper, while the other shot went wide and hit the liquor shelf behind him, smashing half a dozen bottles. Both guns are the same make and model, and have the prints of both men. There is no way of identifying who was carrying which gun, and who fired the fatal shot. The two boys swap guns all the time, and even they don't know which of them fired the fatal shot.

Both Nate and Danny will go down for the crime, but the one guilty of the murder will get life. The police want to pin the murder on one of the two, rather than risking a jury deciding that there is insufficient evidence to convict either, and finding both guilty of a lesser charge. The police offer both men a plea bargain, hoping that one will implicate the other.

What should the two friends do?

Games people play

The prisoner's dilemma is an illustration of game theory devised by mathematicians Merrill Flood (1908–1991) and Melvin Dresher (1911–1992). It explores how 'rational' people behave in situations when co-operation would be mutually beneficial and analyses why, in certain circumstances, they to do not co-operate as expected, and both individuals suffer as a result.

There are four possible solutions to this modified version of the dilemma:

- Nate and Danny implicate one another, and the jury has to decide who to believe. Each faces a fifty–fifty chance of being found guilty and being sentenced to life in prison.
- One confesses to the crime and gets life, while the other remains silent.
- One implicates the other, who decides to remain silent and gets life.
- Both remain silent, and as the jury cannot apportion blame, they are both let off the murder charge.

In ethical terms, you can argue about the relative value of self-interest and altruism, but the people who are most ethically compromised turn out to be the police, because they don't care who gets the rap, as long as someone does. As upholders of the law, they must ensure that the right person is convicted of the murder and receives the appropriate punishment.

THERE IS NO WAY OF KNOWING WHICH ONE OF YOU IS GUILTY, BUT BY SELLING OUT YOUR FRIEND, YOU COULD ENSURE A LESSER PUNISHMENT FOR YOURSELF. WOULD LOYALTY STOP YOU?

♦092 FOOD FOR THOUGHT

You and four friends have gone spelunking in one of the country's largest and least-explored underground cave networks. Despite the best preparations and the latest technology, you are trapped deep underground by a landslide. You know help will come as soon as your party is missed, but with several hundred feet of rubble between you and a rescue team, help may not come in time to save you. You have access to underground water, so will not die of thirst, but your emergency rations will soon be exhausted, and there is a very real likelihood that you will starve to death.

You have a fair idea of how long it might take the rescue team to reach the collapsed tunnel and excavate a small opening through which they could pass supplies. Your best guess is that you will starve to death a week to ten days before help can reach you.

YOU AND FOUR FRIENDS ARE TRAPPED WITH LITTLE HOPE OF IMMEDIATE RESCUE, AND YOU MAY ALL STARVE TO DEATH. WOULD YOU KILL AND EAT SOMEONE TO STAY ALIVE?

The Speluncean Explorers

'The Case of the Speluncean Explorers' was devised by legal philosopher Lon Fuller (1902–1978) in 1949. In Fuller's scenario, the men decide to kill one of their number and eat him to survive, choosing the victim by the roll of a pair of dice. Although the person who suggested the idea and owned the dice changes his mind, the other four go ahead with the scheme and roll for him. He loses but admits that the roll was fair. They kill him, are rescued and are tried for murder, found guilty and sentenced to death. The article explores the verdicts of the six members of a fictional Supreme Court, who take different viewpoints: to uphold the convictions, to set them aside and to take no decision at all.

Survival of the luckiest

The decisions of the justices can be justified using consequentialist, deontological and virtue-ethics arguments. But if we look at the dilemma from the point of view of the spelunkers, what are their ethical choices?

- If you do nothing, then you all die – noble, but selfish, considering you all have partners, families and friends. The death of one is surely preferable to the death of all five (consequentialist). Of course, if you are all executed for murder, you will all die, but at least you can hope for clemency.
- Only one person commits the murder. However, in most jurisdictions, the onlookers, by failing to prevent the crime, are accessories who could be liable for the same penalty.
- One of the party volunteers to die, but there is no way he can kill himself. He suggests that you tie him up and allow him to die of thirst. You are not killing him but letting him die, and you could use the double-effect argument in your defence: his death was foreseen but not intended. That is unlikely to work in a court of law, but you will not have committed first-degree murder.

⚡093 KILLER INSTINCT

RMS *Titanic* has gone down and you and another survivor are nowhere near any of the lifeboats. No, you are not that famous pair of star-crossed lovers, you are two complete strangers, but let's call you Jack and Rose, to pick names completely at random. Your only chance of survival is to find a piece of wreckage large enough that it will not only support your weight but keep you out of the freezing water, which will otherwise kill you in minutes.

You spot a piece of floating debris ahead of you – a large plank of wood that seems to be the only suitable piece of flotsam in the vicinity. The problem is, the other person has also seen it and is making a beeline for it. Being slightly closer, the other person gets there first and claims the plank. Unfortunately, when you yourself reach the plank, you realise it is just large enough to bear the weight of one passenger clear of the water. If you clung to it, you would condemn both of you to death. You have minutes before the icy water makes you too weak to do anything and you drown. What are your options?

Like the other dilemmas included in this section, the situation seems extremely far-fetched, which of course it is. Unfortunately, humans have been put in all these situations at one time or another, and quite a few have survived to tell the tale and be judged for their actions by a jury of their peers.

IF YOU HAD TO KILL SOMEONE SO THAT YOU COULD SURVIVE, COULD YOU ARGUE THAT THE MURDER WAS, IN FACT, AN ACT OF SELF-DEFENCE?

The Plank of Carneades

The ancient Greek sceptic philosopher Carneades of Cyrene (second century CE) devised the scenario above as a thought experiment that has become known as the 'Plank of Carneades', which is cheekily combined here with the plot of a well-known film. Carneades wanted to explore the ethical relationship between murder and self-defence, but not the usual case of self-defence, which would entail you killing an attacker who would otherwise kill you or someone you had the ability to protect (which would not be classed as murder in any case).

If upon reaching the plank, Rose pulls Jack off and he drowns, and she is later rescued by a returning lifeboat, Carneades asks, has she committed the crime of murder for which she can be tried and, in 1912, executed, or because she had to pull Jack off the plank in order to save her own life, is it a case of self-defence?

It would certainly make an interesting legal case. Though, given the circumstances, it would be extremely unlikely that Rose would own up to pulling Jack into the water. She could call upon the double-effect defence, claiming that she could foresee his death but had not intended it. After all, the lifeboat could have come in time to save him. It could explain why she casts the Heart of the Ocean into the sea – to atone for her callous murder.

'*Arms in the hands of citizens may be used at individual discretion for the defense of the country, the overthrow of tyranny, or private self-defense.*'
– **John Adams (1735–1836)**

RELIGION

'Religion is the sigh of the oppressed creature, the heart of a heartless world, and the soul of soulless conditions. It is the opium of the people.'
– Karl Marx (1818–1883)

⚬ 094 SUFFERING FOR HAPPINESS

Dan, a super-rich man of the current generation, has a daughter called Candida. He decides that he will give her the best care and upbringing possible so that she grows up not only well balanced and healthy, but happy. In order to realise his plan, he creates Utopia, a model community with the best facilities that anyone could wish for.

Everything is free for residents as long as they follow a certain number of rules. They must never display any form of illness or unhappiness in public and especially in front of his daughter; if they fall gravely or terminally ill, they must leave Utopia, and the upper age limit for residents is set at forty-five. There is no crime, public disorder or violence, and the information coming in from the outside world is strictly controlled to avoid mention of death, illness, crime, violence, and war. As far as Candida is concerned, she lives in 'the best of all possible worlds'.

> UTILITARIAN PHILOSOPHIES SEEK TO MAXIMISE HAPPINESS AND WELL-BEING AND MINIMISE UNHAPPINESS AND SUFFERING, BUT WHAT IF SUFFERING IS REALLY THE KEY TO A MORE FULFILLED LIFE?

But when Candida turns sixteen, she is no longer satisfied with the limited horizons of Utopia. Yearning to see what the rest of the world is like, she drives out of town unaccompanied for the first time in her life. A few hours later, she arrives at the nearest large town. Driving through one of its disadvantaged neighbourhoods, she sees in turn a frail elderly woman being mugged; a down and out, covered in sores and filth; and finally, a car crash in which the driver of one car is killed.

Four truths, eightfold ethical path

Many readers will recognise in Candida's tale an updated version of the life of the Buddha, Siddhartha Gautama (fifth century BCE), who lived his young years sheltered from the world in a royal palace. Seeing old age, disease and death for the first time, he decided to abandon the luxury of his early life so that he could discover how he could obtain true happiness. After many years of study, austerities and contemplation, he understood the nature of human existence, which he encapsulated in the Four Noble Truths:

1. Life is suffering.
2. Suffering has a cause.
3. The causes of suffering can be overcome.
4. There is a path to ending suffering.

Ending suffering is achieved by following the Eightfold Path:

1. Right Speech
2. Right Action
3. Right Livelihood
4. Right Effort
5. Right Mindfulness
6. Right Concentration
7. Right View
8. Right Intention

Buddhist ethics are not dependent on an all-powerful divinity in the sky with a big stick to keep people in line. Buddhists believe that Godhead is the underlying reality, of which we, like all other manifestations of the material world, form a part. There is no concept of sin, punishment or hell. If we suffer, it is because we do not apprehend the true nature of reality and consciousness. With understanding comes enlightenment, that is, liberation from human suffering and communion with Godhead.

⸞095 RENDER UNTO CAESAR

You are the founding father or mother of a new country, and it is your job to draft the country's constitution, which will define the form of government and its relationship to religion. The majority of the country's population follow one religious faith, but there are also sizeable minorities of other faiths or of no faith at all.

Casting around for inspiration, you study the government of three countries with very different approaches to the issue of church and state: Iran, the United Kingdom and the United States.

Case 1: The Iranian model

The Islamic Republic of Iran is ostensibly a democracy with an elected parliament and president, but they are not sovereign. The real power resides in a ruling council of religious leaders, who have the power to veto any legislation. The state is subject to Islamic law, which makes non-belief a crime and belief in other religions a serious disadvantage. Religion dominates every aspect of Iranian life, from codes of dress to foreign policy.

IN MANY COUNTRIES THE REALMS OF RELIGION AND POLITICS ARE HELD TO BE STRICTLY SEPARATE, BUT IN OTHERS, THE SITUATION IS BLURRED OR RELIGION IS SEEN AS INDIVISIBLE FROM THE STATE. WHO'S GOT IT RIGHT?

Case 2: The British model

The ruling British monarch is also the head of the established Church of England (C of E), though subjects are free to hold any faith or none. Although not a significant voice in government policy, the C of E does have some legislative input, as its bishops are members of the House of Lords. The church also has some residual influence because many UK schools begin their day with an 'act of worship', traditionally understood to be Christian, and it has a leading role in many public and private ceremonies.

Case 3: The American model

The US Constitution establishes the absolute separation of church and state. Religion should not influence the conduct of government, and government funds and institutions cannot be used to promote religious belief. Nevertheless, religion plays a significant but unofficial role in politics and other aspects of American life.

Human rights, divine law

If you hold human rights to be paramount, Iran's theocratic government is the most problematic, as it denies the freedoms of conscience and religion. In an all-too-human world, even sincere believers can fall foul of religious law, compromising their rights further, and with no appeal.

The UK's constitutional muddle is less problematic as there is no duty to believe in anything, even if you are an Anglican. However, British citizens are forced to endorse the established Church because it forms such an integral part of the British state. Some of their taxes will be used to upkeep church buildings and pay the salaries of clerics involved in national ceremonies.

The American model seems to be the most human rights-friendly, but while it is in theory, it isn't always in practice. The influence of religion is felt at all levels of government through the influence of religious conservatives.

❦096 GOOD PEOPLE, BAD THINGS

Natural evil: The forest fire
A lightning bolt strikes a tinder-dry tree in a forest and begins a fire. Fanned by the wind, it becomes an inferno moving through the forest. A family is trapped, and when the father tries to drive through the walls of flame, the heat ignites the petrol in the fuel tank, and the family are burned to death.

Moral evil: The suicide bomber
A family of four are on holiday in a foreign country. They are out shopping for souvenirs and presents for friends and family when they decide to take a break at an outdoor cafe in the centre of the city.

A young man stops in front of the cafe. He is oddly dressed for the time of year: It is summer but he's wearing a heavy coat. The last thing the father remembers is seeing the man throw off his coat revealing that his body is covered in packages linked by wires. The man sets off an explosion that kills the mother and daughter outright, and maims the father, who loses a leg. His son is hit in the head by shrapnel and suffers irreparable brain damage.

> FOR MANY, THE EXISTENCE OF EVIL DEMONSTRATES THE NON-EXISTENCE OF GOD. AFTER ALL, IF THE CHRISTIAN GOD IS OMNIPOTENT, OMNISCIENT AND ENTIRELY GOOD, WHY DOES HE ALLOW EVIL TO EXIST IN THE WORLD?

Theodicies

A theodicy is an attempt to reconcile the existence of God and evil. The simplest theodicy claims that God inflicts evil on humans to punish them or correct their behaviour. But it is hard to see why the blameless children in the scenarios above are being punished, or what they will learn when they're dead.

Another theodicy suggests that because God's plan is ineffable, humans can never understand why he allows evil to exist. In fact, it may be necessary for the accomplishment of some greater good. This, however, leaves the door open for people to commit evil acts, justifying them by saying that if God has allowed them, they must be part of his greater plan.

The two most-often quoted Christian theodicies are those of Saint Augustine of Hippo (354–430 CE) and Saint Irenaeus of Lyons (second century CE). Augustine blamed humanity. He believed that creation is perfect and evil was brought into it by the Fall of Adam and Eve. Irenaeus argued that evil exists as a function of free will. If humans are to achieve moral perfection, they must be free to choose its opposite: evil and suffering.

The evidence is plain

American philosopher William Rowe (1931–2015) used the following logical propositions about the existence of evil to deny the existence of an all-powerful, loving and wholly good divinity:

- God could prevent suffering without compromising some greater good or allowing a greater evil.
- If God is omnipotent, omniscient and wholly good, He would act to prevent suffering, unless it compromised some greater good or permitted a greater evil.
- Therefore, an omniscient, all-powerful, wholly good god cannot exist.

℅ 097 BURQINI BAN

A mother and her two young children are enjoying a day out at the beach in the South of France. She is a member of France's large North African Muslim community, and she is covered up on the beach. It's a few days since the mayor of the resort town has enacted a ban on the 'burqini', a modest form of Islamic bathing dress that covers the head and body, leaving only the face, feet and hands exposed on the grounds that it is an offence to French secularism, and provocative after the deadly attacks in France by Islamist terrorists.

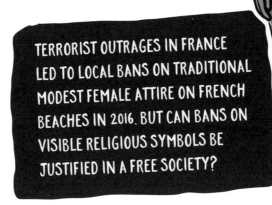

After complaints by fellow beachgoers, the police become involved, issuing the woman with a ticket, and asking her to remove some of her clothing to match the style of dress of other female bathers, who are wearing one-piece swimsuits and bikinis.

France has a long-standing law against the display of conspicuous religious symbols from any faith in public schools, but in recent years, the focus has been on the wearing of the *hijab* (headscarf) and *niqab* (face veil) by Muslim girls and women.

TERRORIST OUTRAGES IN FRANCE LED TO LOCAL BANS ON TRADITIONAL MODEST FEMALE ATTIRE ON FRENCH BEACHES IN 2016. BUT CAN BANS ON VISIBLE RELIGIOUS SYMBOLS BE JUSTIFIED IN A FREE SOCIETY?

Land of *Liberté*?

How does the country that gave the world the stirring rallying cry of '*Liberté, égalité, fraternité*' justify such limitations on the freedoms of religious individuals? In order to understand the bans, one must go back to the French Revolution of 1789 and the disestablishment of the Roman Catholic Church – a battle that was fought and refought bitterly several times until the separation of church and state was enshrined in law in 1905.

For over two centuries it was Christianity and to a lesser extent Judaism that were seen as problematic, and it has only been since the mid-twentieth century and the sizeable increase in the Muslim population that Islam has become the more obvious target of Republican *laïcité* (secularism). Hence, if the French state can be accused of being militantly anti-clerical, historically, it has been very evenhanded about the religions it has discriminated against.

Feminist support

The French left is deeply divided over the ban, but many French feminists support it because they see the wearing of the headscarf and the veil as cultural practices that maintain the oppression of women rather than as genuine religious obligations. They argue that there is a great deal of variation in how 'modest dress' is interpreted across the Islamic world, from full coverage with the *burqa* to the more relaxed *hijab*.

Concern over a woman's hair, however, is not restricted to Islam. Catholic nuns traditionally shave their hair, as do married women of the Jewish Haredi sect, and both would probably wish to adopt a modest style of dress on the beach. However, there seem to be few, if any, similar concerns expressed in France about nuns and Haredi women. As a result, the French leave themselves open to accusations of racism and Islamophobia.

℀098 HOLY WARS

A mighty army sets out on a great holy war to defeat the enemies of God. Thousands of holy warriors leave their homes and fight a series of bloody battles to win a great victory in the name of the One True God. But which One True God? In Biblical times, the Hebrews fought *Milḥemet Mitzvah* in the name of Yahweh; from the eleventh to the seventeenth centuries, Christian knights went on crusade for the greater glory of God; and from the seventh century until the modern period, Muslims have invoked the concept of *jihad* when they have gone to war in the name of Allah.

ONE TRANSLATION OF JIHAD IS 'HOLY WAR', BUT IT HAS OTHER COMPLETELY DIFFERENT MEANINGS. DO WE ACCEPT THE EXTREMISTS' VERSION, OR STRIVE TO UNDERSTAND ITS MORE PEACEFUL INTERPRETATIONS?

Three struggles

The worldwide Islamist outrages since 9/11 have given the West a one-dimensional view of *jihad* as the justification of any act of terror or atrocity committed in the name of Islam, by groups including Al-Qaeda, Al-Shabaab and Daesh (ISIL). The traditional understanding of *jihad*, however, is much more nuanced, and includes the notions of the 'greater' and 'lesser' *jihad*, which can be applied to three different struggles: the inner spiritual struggle of the believer trying to live the good life, the struggle to build an ideal society and a war fought in the defence of Islam.

Greater *jihad*

According to one tradition, the Prophet Muhammad (*c.* 570–632 CE) distinguished the lesser *jihad* – holy war – from the greater *jihad* – the spiritual struggle that believers must win to live true to the faith. A way to fight greater *jihad* is to practice the Five Pillars of Islam (faith, charity, prayer, fasting and pilgrimage to Mecca), and engage in other spiritual and devotional practices, such as learning the Qur'an by heart, cleaning the floor of the mosque, working for social justice, and overcoming anger, greed, hatred, pride and malice.

Lesser *jihad*

The rules that are meant to govern lesser *jihad* are not unlike those of the Christian Just War (see pp. 84–85). Military *jihad* is understood to be a defensive war fought to protect and strengthen Islam, to free Muslims from oppression that prevents them from practising their faith, to protect them from tyranny (even from an unjust Muslim ruler), to punish an oath breaker, and to put right a wrong.

Jihad cannot be fought to forcibly convert people to Islam, to achieve territorial or economic gains, to demonstrate a leader's power, or to settle an international dispute.

In order to be just, *jihad* must be fought against an aggressor, must be launched by a recognised religious authority, must be fought to bring about good, must be a last resort, and must spare non-combatants, especially the aged, children and women. Enemies must be treated justly; the wounded of both sides must receive equal treatment; women must not be raped; and property must not be wantonly damaged.

⚇099 IN THE NAME OF THE FATHER

An elderly couple, Abe and Sarah, are granted a miraculous late birth, promised and delivered by God, even though Sarah is well past the menopause. The birth of Isaac is part of God's covenant with Abe, who will become the father of not one, but two great people: Isaac and his other son Ishmael. Abe's God, however, is not the mellow God of the New Testament. Abe's God destroys whole cities for the transgression of some of their citizens.

Deciding to test Abe's faith, God commands him to banish his elder son, Ishmael, before ordering him to sacrifice his younger son, Isaac. In the most commonly accepted versions of the story, Abe obeys and takes his son atop a mountain with all that they need for a burned offering – except the sacrificial animal. Isaac, who has trudged up a mountain carrying an armful of wood, must be pretty slow on the uptake, as it is only at the summit that he notices there is no animal to sacrifice. In the end, a ram and an angel appear so that Abe, who has proved his faith, does not need to sacrifice Isaac.

ABRAHAM IS REVERED AS THE FOUNDER OF JUDAISM, CHRISTIANITY, AND ISLAM. HE IS THE EXEMPLAR OF MAN'S SUBMISSION TO GOD — WILLING EVEN TO SACRIFICE HIS SON ISAAC. BUT SHOULD ABRAHAM HAVE SAID NO?

Abraham on trial

In *Abraham on Trial* (1998), Carol Delaney (b. 1940) produces a forensic commentary on the Abraham story, examining the religious, cultural and ethical significance of the sacrifice. One theory holds that the story is a rejection of the practice of child sacrifice, but Delaney points out that the Bible doesn't describe such practices being carried out among Abraham's people.

She also questions the automatic assumption on the part of male scholars and commentators that Isaac 'belongs' to Abraham, and is his to sacrifice. Sarah has a stake in her son's life, even in a patriarchal system where the male predominates. And Isaac, too, is an autonomous, sentient being. She also suggests there are alternative versions of the story in which Abraham rebels and does sacrifice Isaac.

Ultimately, Delaney points out that there is no way to reconcile human ethics based on reason and the mystery of faith. She contrasts the attitudes of Danish philosopher Søren Kierkegaard (1813–1855) and arch-rationalist Immanuel Kant. For Kierkegaard, faith and man's submission to it is irrational and above human morality, but Kant disagrees, saying that an immoral command from God must be an illusion.

'Take now thy son, thine only son Isaac, whom thou lovest, and get thee into the land of Moriah; and offer him there for a burned offering upon one of the mountains which I will tell thee of.'
– Genesis 22:2

☙100 JEPHTHAH'S OATH

It is a time of national crisis, with enemies on every side and civil strife. Worse, the people have turned away from the One True God and are worshipping idols and taking part in pagan rites. Displeased, God has turned his back on his chosen people and has allowed their enemies to triumph. Jep has been chosen by his countrymen to lead them at this perilous time.

Jep has a monumental task: He must deal with his enemies, unite his people and square things with God. It's a tough ask for one man, and Jep doesn't entirely feel up to the job. He initially tries diplomacy with the main enemy, but his proposals are rejected. The only recourse is war, but fearing defeat, Jep makes a fatal vow to sacrifice the first thing or person that issues from his house if he returns victorious.

On the fateful day, his daughter comes out to greet him. Jep accepts that he has no choice but to sacrifice his daughter in compliance with his vow.

> JEPHTHAH FOUND HIMSELF WITH AN IMPOSSIBLE DILEMMA AFTER RASHLY SWEARING AN OATH TO GOD. BUT DID HIS DAUGHTER HAVE TO DIE?

Jephthah vs. Abraham

There is a clear parallel between the story of Jephthah and that of Abraham (see previous dilemma), but with a completely different outcome. Here God does not send an angel to save the girl's life. The story is a direct comment on the practice of child sacrifice that was practiced by Israel's pagan neighbours, if not by the Israelites themselves. But if we are to accept this explanation, why does God force Jephthah to go through with an act that he has expressly forbidden?

Jephthah's deontological dilemma is a classic of the genre with absolutely no wriggle room. There are only two possible courses of action: break his oath to God or sacrifice his daughter. Both are moral breaches of equal monstrosity in the eyes of his contemporaries. The sacrifice cannot be seen as an act of faith and submission to God's command, as God did not demand the oath or have any hand in the terms – that is all Jephthah's doing.

It is difficult to see the ethical message contained in the story, though theologians have offered various interpretations: that it demonstrates the danger of unguarded vows; or conversely, that it stresses that oaths are sacred and must be kept at any cost. A more modern interpretation is that, having granted humanity free will, God is allowing Jephthah to exercise it. If that is the case, shouldn't God have given Jephthah a third choice: none of the above?

'Whatever comes out from the doors of my house to meet me when I return in peace from the Ammonites shall be the Lord's, and I will offer it up for a burned offering.'
– **Judges 11:31**

♋101   BET YOUR AFTERLIFE

You are sitting quietly, pondering the existence or non-existence of God (in your case, the Christian god, because your family is Christian). Now in your late fifties, you have less life ahead of you than behind you. Mortality and what comes after death have become more urgent questions.

You have heard many of the arguments in favour of belief: 'Holy Writ' – that the Bible is the revealed word of God. But you know that the Bible was written by men, and there are different versions of the Bible. And what about the other divine revelations?

There is the 'wonders of creation' argument, but, however wonderful, nature could be the product of evolution rather than design. Is the existence of religion and morality a proof of the existence of God? Or are they constructs invented by

THE FRENCH PHILOSOPHER BLAISE PASCAL (1623—1662) MADE THE CASE FOR BELIEVING IN THE EXISTENCE OF GOD IN THE FORM OF A WAGER. WOULD YOU BET FOR OR AGAINST THE EXISTENCE OF GOD?

humans to bring meaning and order to their otherwise absurd lives? Is God to be found in the initial cause of the universe? Something or someone must have set off the Big Bang, or is it an eternal process of innumerable big bangs and big collapses with no first cause?

How are you going to decide what to believe?

Betting for

A kindly looking old man sits next to you and asks what is troubling you. You explain your dilemma. 'Funny you should say that', says the man, introducing himself as Pascal, an itinerant French philosopher. 'I asked myself the same question many years ago.'

Born during the Age of Reason, Pascal was a scientist and mathematician who had long rejected God. An accident in later life made him reconsider his atheism. Having decided that a belief in God could not be established by rationality, Pascal outlined the following solution. He proposed a wager that we all have to make in our lifetime. You can wager for or against the existence of God, but in a wager there must be a stake, winnings and losses. So what's at stake?

If there is a god and you disbelieve, you might profit in your lifetime but then suffer eternal damnation; if there is no God, there will be no punishment or reward, but you might have foregone some material benefits. For Pascal, the prize from betting on the existence of God – a place in heaven – far outweighed betting against his existence – short-term gains and a place in hell. Are you convinced?

Betting against

American philosopher Michael Martin (1932–2015) countered with the Atheist's Wager. The focus of Martin's wager is not on whether you believe or not, but on how you lead your life. If you lead a good life, you are a winner either way, either because God rewards you or you leave a good legacy. If you lead a bad life, you are a loser either way, punished by God or damned by a bad legacy.

FURTHER READING

Anscombe, Elizabeth. *Intention.* Harvard, MA: Harvard University Press, 2000.

Aquinas, Thomas. *Thomas Aquinas: Selected Writings.* Edited by Ralph McInerny. London, UK: Penguin Classics, 1999.

Aristotle. *Ethics.* Translated by W. D. Ross. London, UK: Create Space Independent Publishing Platform, 2016.

Asimov, Isaac. *I, Robot.* New York, NY: Spectra Books, 2008.

Austin, John L. *How to Do Things with Words: The William James Lectures delivered at Harvard University in 1955.* Edited by J. O. Urmson and Marina Sbisà. Oxford, UK: Harvard University Press,1962.

Beauchamp, Tom and Childress, James. *Principles of Biomedical Ethics.* New York, NY: Oxford University Press, USA, 2013.

De Beauvoir, Simone. *The Second Sex.* London, UK: Vintage Classics, 1997.

Bentham, Jeremy. *An Introduction to the Principles of Morals and Legislation.* London, UK: Dover Publications, 2007.

Bloom, Allan. *The Closing of the American Mind.* New York, NY: Simon & Schuster, 1987.

Butler, Judith. *Gender Trouble.* London, UK: Routledge, 2006.

Carens, Joseph. *The Ethics of Immigration.* Oxford, UK: Oxford University Press, 2015.

Delaney, Carol. *Abraham on Trial: The Social Legacy of Biblical Myth.* Princeton, NJ: Princeton University Press 1998.

Dworkin, Andrea. *Pornography.* New York, NY: The Women's Press Ltd., 1989.

Finlay, Christopher. *Terrorism and the Right to Resist: A Theory of Just Revolutionary War.* Cambridge, UK: Cambridge University Press: 2015.

Foot, Philippa. *Moral Dilemmas: And Other Topics in Moral Philosophy.* Oxford, UK: Oxford University Press, 2003.

Foucault, Michel. *The History of Sexuality, Vol. I: The Will to Knowledge.* London, UK: Penguin, 1998.

_____. *The History of Sexuality, Vol. II: The Use of Pleasure.* London, UK: Vintage Books, 1990.

_____. *The History of Sexuality, Vol III: The Care of the Self.* London, UK: Vintage Books, 1990.

Fuller, Lon. *The Morality of Law.* New Haven, CT: Yale University Press, 1969.

Goulet, Denis. *The Cruel Choice: A New Concept in the Theory of Development.* New York, NY: Atheneum Press, 1971.

Greer, Germaine. *The Female Eunuch.* New York, NY: Harper Perennial Modern Classics, 2008.

Hooker, Brad. *Ideal Code, Real World: A Rule-Consequentialist Theory of Morality.* New York, NY: Oxford University Press, USA, 2003.

Kant, Immanuel. *Critique of Pure Reason.* London, UK: Penguin Classics, 2007.

_____. *The Moral Law: Groundwork of the Metaphysics of Morals.* London, UK: Routledge Classics, 2005.

Kenny, Anthony. *A New History of Western Philosophy.* Oxford, UK: Oxford University Press, 2012.

Lin, Patrick; Abney, Keith and Bekey, George (eds). *Robot Ethics: The Ethical and Social Implications of Robotics.* Cambridge, MA: MIT Press, 2011.

Machiavelli, Niccolò. *The Prince.* London, UK: Penguin Classics, 2003.

MacKinnon, Catherine. *Women's Lives, Men's Laws.* Harvard, MA: Harvard University Press, 2007.

Martin, Michael. *Atheism: A Philosophical Justification*. Philadelphia, PA: Temple University Press, 1989.

McGee, Robert. *The Ethics of Tax Evasion*. New York, NY: Springer Science & Business Media, 2011.

Mill, John Stuart. *On Liberty, Utilitarianism and Other Essays*. Oxford, UK: Oxfrod Univerity Press, 2015.

Mills, Nicolaus. *Debating Affirmative Action*. New York, NY: Delta, 1994.

Næss, Arne. *Ecology, Community, and Lifestyle: Outline of an Ecosophy*. Cambridge, UK: Cambridge University Press: 1989.

Nozick, Robert. *Anarchy, State and Utopia*. London, UK: Wiley-Blackwell, 2001.

Nussbaum, Martha and Sen, Amartya. *The Quality of Life*. Oxford, UK: Oxford University Press, 1993.

Orend, Brian. *The Morality of War*. Peterborough, UK: Broadview Press, 2006.

Orwell, George. *1984*. New York, NY: Signet Classic, 1961.

Pascal, Blaise. *Pensées*. Translated by A. J. Krailsheimer. London, UK: Penguin Classics, 1995.

Rachels, James. *The Elements of Moral Philosophy*. London, UK: McGraw-Hill Education, 2014.

Regan, Tom. *The Case for Animal Rights*. Oakland, CA: University of California Press, 2004.

Rollin, Bernard. *Animal Rights and Human Morality*. Amherst, MA: Prometheus Books, 2006.

Rowe, William. *Philosophy of Religion: An Introduction*. Belmont, CA: Wadsworth Publishing, 1978.

Russell, Bertrand. *Marriage and Morals*. London, UK: Liveright, 1970.

Ryder, Richard. *God and the Problem of Evil*. London, UK: Blackwell, 2001.

Savulescu, Julian and Bostrom, Nick. *Human Enhancement*. New York, NY: Oxford University Press, USA, 2011.

Sen, Amartya Kumar. *Inequality Reexamined*. Oxford, UK: Clarendon Press, 1995.

Sher, George (ed). *Utilitarianism*. Indianapolis, IN: Hackett Publishing, 2002.

Sher, George. *Who Knew? Responsibility Without Awareness*. Oxford, UK: Oxford University Press, 2009.

Singer, Peter. *Animal Liberation*. London, UK: Bodley Head, 2015.

_____. *The Most Good You Can Do: How Effective Altruism is Changing Ideas About Living Ethically*. New Haven, CT: Yale University Press, 2015.

_____. *The Life You Can Save: How to Play Your Part in Ending World Poverty*. London, UK: Random House, 2010.

Soulé, Michael. *Conservation Biology: The Science of Scarcity and Diversity*. Sunderland, MA: Sinaver Associates, 1986.

Szasz, Thomas. *The Myth of Mental Illness: Foundations of a Theory of Personal Conduct*. New York, NY: Harper Perennial, 2010.

Thomson, Judith. *Rights, Restitution, and Risk: Essays in Moral Theory*. Harvard, MA: Harvard University Press, 1986.

Unger, Peter. *Living High and Letting Die: Our Illusion of Innocence*. Oxford, UK: Oxford University Press, 1996.

Walzer, Michael. *Just and Unjust Wars: A Moral Argument with Historical Illustrations*. New York, NY: Basic Books, 2015.

Warren, Mary Anne. *Moral Status: Obligations to Persons and Other Living Things*. Oxford, UK: Oxford University Press, 2000.

Williams, Bernard. *Moral Luck: Philosophical Papers 1973–1980*. Cambridge, UK: Cambridge University Press, 1981.

Willis, Ellen. *The Essential Ellen Willis*. Edited by Nona Willis Aronowitz. Minneapolis, MN: University of Minnesota Press, 2014.

✦ INDEX